LIVING FAITH
WHILE
HOLDING DOUBTS

UPDATED

LIVING FAITH
WHILE
HOLDING DOUBTS

UPDATED

Martin B. Copenhaver

THE
PILGRIM
PRESS
Cleveland

To Karen
whose love keeps me going and
whose questions keep me honest

The Pilgrim Press,
700 Prospect Avenue, Cleveland, Ohio 44115

© 2013 by Martin B. Copenhaver
©1989 by The Pilgrim Press

Scripture quotations, unless otherwise noted, are from the New Revised Standard Version of the Bible, © 1989 by the Division of Christian Education of the National Council of Churches of Christ in the United States of America and are used by permission.

Portions of chapter 7 are based on "The Word Gets Around" by Martin B. Copenhaver. Copyright 1985 Christian Century Foundation. Reprinted by permission from the May 1985 issue of *The Christian Ministry*.

Library of Congress Cataloging-in-Publication Data
Copenhaver, Martin B., 1954–
    Living faith while holding doubts / Martin B. Copenhaver.
      p. cm.
    ISBN 978-0-8298-1990-8 (updated edition, 2013)
    ISBN 0-8298-0798-5 (pbk. : alk. paper)
    1. Faith.   2. Belief and doubt.   I. Title.
  BT774.C67   1988
  234' .2–dc19   88-7552

Contents

Foreword

A GREAT DEAL HAS CHANGED since *Living Faith While Holding Doubts* was first published in 1989. Today religion is more likely to be associated—in the popular mind and public perception—with violence, terrorism, or extremism. In 2001, radical Islamists were responsible for the 9/11 attacks on the United States, but the linkage is not limited to Islam. It can also be found in Christianity. In 1995, the Oklahoma City bombing linked some variety of Christianity to domestic terrorism. Sadly, many more such incidents tying religion and violence could be listed. One thing that has changed, then, is that in the popular mind, religion and violent extremism are much more frequently associated.

There have been other shifts—seismic ones—in this period. America is no longer the Protestant Christian nation that it has been, at least by some measures. As late as 1983, 78 percent of Americans self-identified as Protestant Christian. By 2008, according to the Pew Research Center, that percentage had fallen to 51 percent. Protestantism—whether Evangelical or mainline—no longer enjoys the "taken-for-granted" status that was so long the case in North America. Moreover, the 2010 census confirmed what many had suspected: The fastest growing category, religiously speaking, are the so-called "Nones," those who indicate "none" when asked about religious affiliation.

Much has changed in recent decades in North America, particularly with regard to the role and place of religion in general, and Christianity in particular. Many of these changes have sown new seeds of doubt and distrust. But not all the changes are so self-evidently negative. A 2008 Gallup Poll confirmed that while interest in church attendance has declined, interest in "spirituality" has grown. This is evidenced by the

now ubiquitous use of the phrase "spiritual but not religious."
While such terms tend to hide at least as much as they reveal,
these counter-trends indicate that interest in the spiritual
life—even longing for spiritual meaning—is as strong, perhaps
even stronger, than in a previous era.

So as we note major shifts of the last quarter century—the
association of religion with violence, the decline of Protestant
hegemony, the increased interest in spirituality—what are
the implications for the present volume? For this observer,
the relevance of *Living Faith While Holding Doubts* has only
grown with the passage of time since its initial publication.
Both doubts about faith and religion and interest in faith
and religion are—perhaps paradoxically—abundant. Martin
Copenhaver has written a book for such a time as this, a time
of doubt and a time of longing.

If much larger social context has changed during the
period between the first and second editions of *Living Faith
While Holding Doubts,* there is, nevertheless, also continuity. One instance of that continuity is in the interests, even
the passions, of its author, Martin Copenhaver. His central
interests and commitments are constant. They are the interests and commitments of a pastoral theologian, and accord-
ingly, *Living Faith While Holding Doubts* is a work of pastoral
theology.

It is a work concerned with the core questions that pastors
should address in the practice of ministry. This might itself be
described as the "care and the cure of souls." These have been
the abiding interests and passions of Pastor Copenhaver, as
evidenced by his other books and articles as well as his ministry as a congregational pastor and teacher over a period of
more than thirty years. His focus has been clear and consistent: helping people and congregations to grow in faith.

One might think that this would be the primary focus of all ordained ministers, especially those serving congregations. But that is not the case. Whether through timidity or distraction or lack of vocational clarity, many clergy seem not to get to the heart of the matter, to what Jesus said to Mary and Martha: that "one thing needful," a living faith.

Copenhaver, however, is focused on this central concern of ministry and the church: growing people of faith, of which this book is evidence. He addresses the questions people—both those within the church and those who are not within the church—are asking about faith, its meaning, and its significance.

Moreover, he focuses on these essential matters with wisdom born of a mind and spirit alert to—not averse to—complexity. For when it comes to such terms and experiences as "belief," "faith," and "doubt," there can be no simple or easy answers. As one example of his alertness to complexity consider the following brief excerpt in which he explores the relative merits the terms of "growth" versus "decision." Is faith something that grows gradually and over time? Or are there decisive moments, times to decide and commit? Here's Copenhaver:

> What is often lost in drawing such distinctions is that it poses a false choice. Both decision and growth have a place in relationships, including our own relationship with God. This is easy to observe in matters of the heart. There is a place for the slow flowering of a love, but there is also a place for the decision to marry. We may not be able to decide to love someone, but we can decide to commit ourselves to the one we have begun to love.

One's marginalia at such a point—indeed on the entire book—might be "Pay Attention: Pastor at Work."

Today there are two particular types of people for which I think this book will prove deeply helpful. One is the long-time church member who wonders now what she or he really believes, if anything. Under the pressure of changes noted earlier—the association of religion with violent extremism, the diminished role of Protestant Christianity, an increased interest in spirituality—some who were once more ardent find themselves living today with a diminished faith. This book honors where they are, but does not leave them there.

The second person for whom I can imagine this book to be especially welcome is what we have learned to call "the seeker." The number of "un-," "under-" and "de-churched" people in all our communities is growing. The number of those who have little or no church experience is on the increase. Some of those, at least, are eager to find a congregation where their questions, including their doubts, can be explored in safety and with others who seek to live their faith while holding doubts. For such seekers, and the congregations that wish to welcome them, this book will be especially valuable.

Anthony B. Robinson
Eastertide, 2013

Preface

THIS BOOK IS NOT FOR EVERYONE. This book is not for those who are free from the grip of doubt. It is not for those who have found belief in God easy. It is not for those who have had an experience of belief that is so compelling that they are convinced, with Saint Teresa, that one drop of it, falling on hell, would turn hell into paradise. There are such people, to be sure, whose belief is so luminous and constant that it defies every shadow and seems to banish the night. There are a few such people, but there are very few indeed.

Neither is this book for those who are utter disbelievers. It is not for those who are confirmed and comfortable in their disbelief in God. It is not for those who have determined that religion is simply a numbing tonic of superstition and wishful thinking. There are such people, as surely as there are constant believers, who have concluded that stories of God are mere fairy tales, relics of childhood that are unbecoming, if not downright harmful, if carried into adulthood. There are such people, but their number is not as large as is sometimes supposed.

This book is addressed to those who find themselves between these two groups. They have neither luminous belief nor utter disbelief. They can affirm a belief in God, on occasion at least, yet still hold doubts and never quite get used to the uneasy mix of doubt and belief in their lives. Their belief is hesitant, uncertain, sporadic, often unsatisfying. They may yearn for belief, yet find it elusive. The words of the man who turned to Jesus echo in their own hearts: "I believe; help my unbelief" (Mark 9:24).

Although much of what is said in this book pertains to the relationship between belief and doubt in general, it is addressed more specifically to those who both believe and disbelieve what the Christian tradition affirms about God. It is written for those who may have considerable doubt about many things, including the claims made by other world religions, but whose experience of doubting the Christian God is somehow different. For these readers, what is affirmed in the Christian tradition may be just as hard to accept as other claims to truth, but it is not rejected with the same ease with which other claims are rejected or at least not without a certain wistful reluctance. It is to the Christian gospel that they return again and again, even if they bring the same doubt with them each time.

Those who have such a mixture of belief and disbelief may be found outside the church, but, just as surely, they can be found within the church. Such people may choose to remain on the fringe of the church's life, but may also be found among the active and involved. They may attend worship each Sunday. They may teach Sunday school. They may be deacons. And—need I add—they may be ordained ministers as well.

I think of one such person I will call David. It is a Sunday morning. David walks up the worn and familiar steps of his church. He is greeted by a cheery cluster of members chatting in the narthex. Someone asks him why he brought an umbrella. He replies that he brought it along to ensure that it would not rain that day. It is an old joke they have shared on many occasions, but everyone laughs anyway. The joke and the laughter are among the Sunday rituals that have been worn smooth through time.

David is ushered to his seat. And it is *his* seat. Ever since he joined the church he has sat in the same pew. When, on occasion, it has been filled and he has been forced to sit elsewhere, he has had to fight a feeling of resentment, almost as if he had entered his home to find someone else living there.

Almost from the moment he sits down David feels a certain restless discomfort. He knows the sources of his discomfort well enough. He has brought something with him that he is convinced does not belong there, something he wishes he could have left in the narthex along with his umbrella. But despite his best efforts, it is there. Uninvited. Unwelcome. Undeniable. Doubt.

The doubts he brings cause a discomfort that is as familiar as everything around him in church, but today the doubts seem more rude and nagging. He can usually put his doubts aside long enough to participate in worship, and, on occasions at least, he has been able to sense something like the presence of God. But the doubts that merely whispered in his mind on other occasions are today given full voice and cannot be ignored. At every turn in the worship service they seem to demand attention.

David joins the congregation in saying the opening prayer, but even before the words "Dear God" escape his lips, his mind is overcome with the shadow of doubt because that is all he hears—words, hollow and lifeless. The scripture reading, about Jesus dividing the fish and loaves to feed the five thousand, strikes him as more than just a little odd. In the past he has heard interpretations of the story that stressed its spiritual meaning rather than its historical accuracy, but on this occasion the very implausibly of the story seems to obliterate any meaning at all. During the moment of silent prayer his efforts to pray feel like trying to get the car started on a cold winter's morning. No amount of effort or coaxing will get the prayer started. He listens to the sermon, but the words of the preacher, and in fact that whole Christian story, strike him as quite unlikely, if not downright bizarre. He sneaks a look around and notices that everyone around him seems perfectly calm. No one appears in the least agitated by the bizarre nature of the story being told. There are no quizzical looks. He turns again to the preacher and wishes that, just once, he could crawl inside the preacher's mind to determine if he believes all that he is saying. When David stands with the congregation to recite a creed, the words, as familiar as the names of loved ones, stick on his tongue. The final hymn fills the church, but the very resonance of the music prompts David to wonder: Does this song of praise resonate so beautifully because it is merely bouncing off the ceiling of the church, as all the prayers and hymns and praises have bounced off the ceiling, because it has no other place to go?

After worship David picks up his umbrella and heads for his car. As he walks, some of the words he has heard during the worship come back to him again like a murmuring mob, words like "God," "savior," "miracle." The words are mingled with another sound, the sound of little exclamation points dropping all around him. It has begun to rain.

I have never met David, except in my imagination. And yet in another way I know I have met him a thousand times. After all, he has as many names as there are people who both believe and disbelieve, who can affirm faith and yet still hold doubts. David may be known in a variety of circumstances and by a number of names, but a day does not pass that I do not meet him. I say this with certainly because one of the names he goes by is my own.

The manner in which belief and doubt are mixed in each person's life is as individual as an autograph. Yet this book is addressed to the common experience of those who find the two inextricably mixed. The aim is not to dispel all doubt, because that is not something that this book, or any other, can achieve. Furthermore, the aim is not to make us comfortable with our doubts. Such efforts always end up sounding glib. When we experience that looming and difficult reality of doubt, words of easy comfort become woefully inadequate. If we are to approach the subject of doubt honestly and helpfully, we must do so with the respect with which we might approach the ocean, aware of its power and mindful of the threat it can pose. In the face of such a reality, glib words and easy reassurances can be misleading, if not dangerous.

The aim of this book, then, is to assign doubt to its proper place within the life of faith. To put the matter bluntly: Now that we have these doubts, what are we going to do with them? And how will we know when doubts have been assigned to their proper place? It will not be when those doubts cease to have urgency for us or when we get used to them or become comfortable in their presence. Quite simply, we will know when doubts have been assigned to their proper place when those doubts do not prevent us from acting on the belief we do have. And if we are successful, if our doubts are assigned to a place where they can still sting but no longer debilitate us, if we do not settle comfortably into our doubts any more than we can settle comfortably into our belief, then we will discover something else, a blessed irony: Those very doubts have the power to deepen and enrich our relationship with God as nothing else can.

LIVING FAITH
WHILE
HOLDING DOUBTS

CHAPTER ONE

Trying to Learn Belief

WE SOMETIMES SPEAK as if there are two kinds of people: those who believe in God and those who do not. But such clear distinctions are only rarely reflected in life. In life as we experience it, the distinction between the believer and the doubter is not so easily made. Even the most ardent believer has moments of entertaining doubts. And the most confirmed skeptic has moments when his or her doubts are themselves subject to doubt.

In our own lives there may be times when belief in God suddenly asserts itself as robust and strong, even times when belief seems almost easy. There are other times when God seems not only distant but unreal, times when doubt casts such a long shadow that it darkens even the recollection of times when we believed. Most often, perhaps, doubt and belief are found together as constant companions within us, each making its loud claims, each arguing against the other. And so we cry out over the inner debate between belief and doubt with the plea one desperate man addressed to Jesus: "I believe; help my unbelief" (Mark 9:24).

We may be quite familiar with the way in which belief and doubt cling to each other like tired boxers, but we can never get used to it. We would send doubt away defeated if we could. At the very least we would like to increase our belief and decrease our doubt. And so we seek help in diminish our doubts and wonder where such help might be found.

The question that hovers around our longing is this: Can we learn to believe? Put another way, is belief an achievement?

Is there anything we can do to find belief, or are we condemned merely to wait in helpless longing for a belief that remains elusive?

Initial responses to these questions are bound to be disappointing. Clearly, belief in God is not learned in the same way as, say, mathematics is learned. Any person with some intelligence can be taught to add, if given proper instruction. Adding might come quickly to some and slowly to others. It might seem almost effortless to some and an arduous task to others, but eventually the result will be the same. All will eventually learn how to add. This is not true of belief. In religious education of equally intelligent, equally diligent, equally good people, some will respond with belief and others with disbelief.

All over the world people are taught the Christian religion. Certainly this instruction is not entirely fruitless, but we should be clear about what we can expect such instruction to achieve. Through instruction and study people can learn about the Christian religion. They can learn about what is said in the Bible. They can learn about the practices of the church. They can learn about Christian theology. They can even learn about belief.

Nevertheless, this learning "about" the Christian religion is very different from learning belief. People can acquire a masterful grasp of what is said in the Bible without assenting to it. They can learn in detail the manifold practices of the church without participating in any of them. They can exhibit an impressive understanding of theological statements about God without ever having to grant that there is a God. They can learn about all these things without ever believing any of them.

People can learn about the Christian religion as they can learn about any religion, through instruction and study. But even the most rigorous instruction and careful study will not teach belief. People can be taught about belief without ever learning to believe. As John Westerhoff III has observed, "Sometimes even when the [church] school has succeeded, it has only produced educated atheists."[1]

To use an image employed by Søren Kierkegaard, one can read the Bible, or the whole Christian tradition, as one might read a guidebook to a country one has never visited. It can even be read by those who never intend such a visit—read not as a useful tool but as a mere amusement or detached intellectual exercise. One can learn about the foreign land of belief without ever getting the dirt of that land on one's shoes.

There are others, however, who would be willing to travel to the land of belief on a moment's notice if they knew how to get there. Their bags are already packed. Those who seek to believe may be momentarily encouraged when they hear that there are several philosophical "proofs" of the existence of God. This is especially true when they discover that such "proofs" have occupied the greatest minds of Western civilization, beginning before the birth of Christ with the philosophy of Plato. Through the centuries these so-called proofs have been reformulated, even refined, and they remain a source of great interest for many in our day. Indeed, if such proofs of the existence of God were ultimately satisfying, it would be important for us to put all else aside to consider them. But, unfortunately, this is not the case. As it is, a brief look at one such proof will be sufficient here. [2]

Proofs of the Existence of God

This one proof of the existence of God is cited often and in a variety of contexts. It has been presented in sophisticated forms by some of the great philosophers of history. In fact, it has been cited so often in philosophical circles that a philosophical name, the "teleological proof," has been bestowed upon it. But it is also worth considering because, in its simpler variations, it has had the most appeal for ordinary people. People untutored in the language and methods of philosophy often make reference to it in common discourse (but, of course, without referring to it by name). Briefly the teleological proof concludes that there is a God by pointing out the design and purposefulness of creation. The proof begins by observing the inherent order and delicate balance of the world. Whenever we use the wonder of the world as reason to conclude there is a Creator behind it all, we are using a form of the teleological proof. When we marvel at the bold splashes of color in a sunset dancing on the waters of a wooded lake or stand in reverent awe before the human ability to reason or feel, and conclude from these things that there must be a Creator God behind it all, then, whether we are aware of it or not, we are using a form of this proof.

Some forms of this proof are tightly reasoned. Others are more poetic. An example of the latter was offered by Harry Emerson Fosdick when he asked in a sermon,

> All the law-abiding order and beauty of the world, all the nobility of human character at its best, explained as though the physical letters of the alphabet had been blown together by a chance wind into the Thirteenth Chapter of First Corinthians? Christ himself and all he stands for, nothing, as it were, nothing but the physical notes of the musical scale tossed by purposeless winds until accidentally they fell together into the Ninth Symphony of Beethoven? Is that not utterly incredible? Are you not bound to doubt your doubts?[3]

One of the appealing aspects of this proof of the existence of God is that it is not shaken by new advances and discoveries in the field of science. Instead, this proof seems actually to gain more evidence as science increases its range of vision to reveal the ever more stunning richness and detail in creation. For instance, we now know that the molecules in one drop of water, if magnified to the size of a grain of sand, would furnish enough sand to cover the whole of the United States with a sand bank fifty feet deep. It has been estimated that the proton in an atom is about 1/400,000,000 of an inch in diameter. The electron has its own kind of "solar system," traveling 10,000 miles per second within a spherical limit of 1/100,000,000 of an inch. Such findings seem to support our sense that creation follows a complex design indeed. When we consider these things, is it possible to conclude that the world simply came together by chance? Are we not led to conclude that the world is not simply thrown together by chance but rather that it follows the master design of a Creator?

And yet it is here that we must face a disturbing truth about this proof of the existence of God that pertains to the other proofs as well. Quite simply, as intriguing and appealing as these observations may be to us, they cannot properly be called proofs. A proof is something that can be demonstrated and receive universal consent. In a true proof the evidence stands on its own, without outside support. But this cannot be said of the proofs of the existence of God. None of the so-called proofs of the existence of God can be strictly called proofs because they do not have the power to move us from doubt to belief. Proofs of the existence of God are unconvincing to those who have not experienced God in their lives and unnecessary to those who have. When the Soviet cosmonaut Yuri Gagarin came back from space and made the famous statement that he never saw God in heaven, an Orthodox priest in Moscow replied, "If you have not seen him on earth, you will not see him in heaven." Likewise, if we have not experienced the presence of God in our lives, we will not likely see God in any proof.

Those who find in the design and purposefulness of the universe reason to believe in the existence of God are almost always those who already believed before any such proof was offered. Those who did not believe in God before being presented with the evidence will not likely come to believe in God after a consideration of such evidence. A sunset over a lake or a study of the dynamics of an atom will leave believers believing and doubters doubting. Some will see in a beautiful sunset the work of the master Creator while others will see simply a beautiful sunset. While observing the same evidence, very different conclusions are drawn. Evidence may be marshaled on the side of belief or doubt but only in order to support a conclusion that has already been reached, not because of any prior evidence but because of a conviction that precedes any evidence.

Eventually we must conclude that, for both believer and doubter, proofs of the existence of God are quite beside the point. Even if the land of doubt and the land of belief are connected by a bridge of proofs, it is a tenuous bridge that we do not trust to bear the full weight of our lives. If we are to cross the chasm, we must use other means and leave the bridge unused.

If only it were otherwise. Then the task of dispelling our doubts would be simply a matter of fully understanding the evidence. We would be encouraged to study more. We would seek out another, perhaps wiser, instructor. We would want to read just one more edifying book. We would even be willing to sign up for a philosophy course to study the traditional philosophical proofs of God's existence if on the last day of the semester we were granted a belief in God along with our diploma. Unfortunately, none of this is possible. Belief in God is not acquired through instruction or proofs.

But if instruction and proofs cannot lead to belief, it is important to give equal weight to the corollary: Instruction and proof cannot lead away from belief either. It has never been proved that God does not exist, and it cannot be proved. Neither belief nor disbelief can be strictly taught. If God is not discovered at the end of an argument, neither does God disappear at the end of a contrary argument. This understanding is so often lost in our time. Many assume that if we are to believe in the existence of God we must do so in spite of the evidence. Often it is assumed that those who doubt God are relying on the 20/20 vision of reason while those who believe in God are following blind faith. But this is not the case.

Proofs and other forms of conventional instruction do not lead us in either direction, either toward doubt or toward belief. Rather, after all the careful instruction and reasoned discourse, we are left with a choice between two different beliefs: Do we believe that there is a God or do we believe that there is no God? If we marshal all the evidence of God or the opposite, we are left where we were before any evidence or proof was offered: Do we believe in God or do we not?

Proofs of the existence of God may be simply irrelevant for the person who seeks to believe in God, but there is another argument against them that should be briefly noted. The God whose existence each of these proofs aims to establish is finally only a pale shadow of the God described in the Bible and worshiped in the church. For instance, even if we could establish to everyone's satisfaction the existence of an almighty creator God by pointing to the design and order in the universe, that would still leave the vast majority of Christian understandings about God unproved and unprovable. We cannot prove (or disprove) that God established an eternal covenant with the people of Israel. We cannot demonstrate through logic that God spoke to prophets and apostles. We cannot demonstrate through argument that God is both judge and lover of all creation. We cannot establish through mere teaching that God cares for each person individually. We cannot reason our way to believing that the Jesus of history is also the risen Christ. All these central tenants of the Christian faith, and many more, are simply beyond the province of even the most compelling proof of the existence of God. If the biblical depiction of God is a large and elaborate portrait, at their best the proofs are merely the shadow cast by the portrait when it is hung on the wall. From that shadow alone we cannot determine the color of the portrait or its texture. We cannot sense the perspective and depth of what is depicted. Not even an outline of the one portrayed on the canvas can be deduced from the shadow on the wall. We cannot even know from the shadow on the wall if the one depicted in the portrait is good or evil, for, as H. D. Aiken remarked, "Logically, there is no reason why an almighty and omniscient being might not be a perfect stinker."[4]

Our Experience of God

Beyond all this, it is important to consider our doubts in the context in which they usually arise in our lives, which is not in the form of proofs to be considered or logic to be followed. Questions about the existence of God or the essential nature of God do not usually take shape for us in the form of a detached philosophical discussion. Rather, our doubts arise in more immediate and compelling ways out of our own experiences. It is life, not theory, that gives rise to doubt. Indeed, for most people the greatest obstacle to belief is not belief's irrationality but life's injustice.

This obstacle to belief can arise in countless ways, as manifold as the ways of sorrow and tragedy: A woman looks and feels fine, and yet she lives under the threat of a silent enemy, a disease that may not claim her life, but that has already claimed much of the spark and spirit of her life. Her experiences give rise to the question, "Why?" It is a question that implies others: "Who?" and "Where?" and "How?" "Who is God?" And "Where is God in all of this?" And, "How can I believe in God anymore?"

Or a man may look beyond the numbing statistics about homelessness and see a person, one who might be called by some a child of God but who looks more like a forsaken orphan—dirty, bloodshot, unshaven. Yet the person looks in other ways so much like the observer that the observer is led to wonder if the homeless one is just a sad reminder that we are all orphans of an absent or nonexistent God. The question bubbles into consciousness, "Is there no God?"

Anywhere we may look in the human experience there are occasions that raise similar questions of doubt: The promise of a young life is cut off by death; a cherished hope is snuffed out; a life is in tatters; whole peoples are oppressed; evil claims ill-gotten victories; nature is furious and random, leaving destruction in its wake; death comes by inches and we can do nothing but watch. Friendships freeze over; love withers and dies; families, formed and conceived in love, are torn asunder by bitterness and enmity; warring madness is a daily reality for millions and a constant threat to us all. Those who have experienced or witnessed suffering often find that the question staggers out of their incredulous hearts: "Is there indeed a God who cares?"

In such questions we can hear the bitter echo of Job's questions of God: "What are human beings, that you make so much of them, . . . visit them every morning, test them every moment?" (Job 7:17–18). We can hear another question from the psalmist that eventually would be taken up by Jesus himself on the cross, "My God, my God, why have you forsaken me?" (Psalm 22:1 and Matthew 27:46). And, if we are attentive, we can hear fresher voices asking new forms of the old questions, perhaps even in our own voice or the voice of any-one whose experience of sorrow or suffering leads him or her to ask, "Can there really be a God?"

If suffering is the most fertile ground for doubt to grow, then perhaps that offers the key to understanding why some people doubt and others believe. Belief is not something that can be taught, but rather, perhaps, it is learned through expe-rience. If we have lived among loving people who have an intimate concern for our welfare, is it not more likely that our experience will make it easier for us to conceive of a God who knows the very number of hairs on our heads and notes the fall of every sparrow? If our experience has been otherwise, if we have lived amid the darker realities of life, would we not expect that belief in such a God would be difficult? Surely we would expect that someone like Job would find it more diffi-cult to believe in a caring God than someone who had led a seemingly charmed life. It seems reasonable to assume that a child who has lived in the violent streets of Detroit or Bagdad has more ample reason to doubt the existence of an all loving God than the child who was brought up without such fear. A person who is told by a doctor, "There is nothing more we can do," would seem more likely to doubt the existence of a com-passionate and almighty God than would the person for whom a mysterious remission of the disease takes pace.

Upon closer examination, however, this explanation for why some doubt and others believe does not satisfy. For instance, if belief or doubt were dependent on outward cir-cumstances, we would expect that the towering affirmation of belief in the Bible would most likely arise out of the experi-ence of those who lived lives of ease and privilege, free from the usual human quota of hardship. Even the most cursory reading of the Bible, however, reveals something else. The Christian faith was not born out of times when we might think belief would be easy, that is, when life itself is easy, or at least relatively happy and free from hardship. No, the Christian faith was born out of suffering, the suffering of an exiled people, a crucified Lord, and persecuted followers. It arose out of the gritty reality of life as it is really lived, amid hardships, disappointments and grim, circumstances.

Suffering may sometimes prompt doubt, it seems, but the biblical witness demonstrates that we cannot always expect this. In fact, in some instances, the fullest expression of belief can come from those who have known the greatest suffering. It was Job, not any of his blithe and detached comforters, who was able to cry in the end, "I had heard of you by the hearing of the ear, but now my eyes see you" (Job 42:5). When Paul cried, "Who will separate us from the love of Christ?" and went on to list a whole series of calamities, he was not being merely rhetorical. He was speaking as one who has known peril and nakedness and the sword and who had yet discovered that "in all these things we are more than conquerors, through him who loved us" (Romans 8:35–37). And, of course, it was after Jesus spoke his famous words of doubt on the cross that he spoke his last words, words of faith in a triumphant key, "Father, into your hands I commit my spirit" (Luke 23:46).

If suffering is the most profound challenge to belief in God, how is it that some who have suffered so acutely are still able to affirm a full and vital belief? It is certainly not because their belief in God offers a satisfactory answer to the question of why people suffer. Indeed, the biblical authors do not try to explain suffering. No theories are offered on why suffering should be. In the face of real suffering all explanations and theories are inadequate. Those who offer such explanations and theories presume to know more about the way of God than any person is given to know. But even more they do an injustice to those who suffer by refusing to grant the magnitude of suffering, what might be called the dignity of suffering, if it can be so easily explained. Of course, this is not to say that the nature of suffering is not of great concern to those who believe in God. Unexplainable suffering can be a powerful challenge to belief in God, but it does not necessarily lead to doubt. Although suffering remains inexplicable to the person who believes in God, that person may nonetheless believe for reasons that may seem equally mysterious and inexplicable.

The striking presence of such strong and vibrant belief in those who have been beset by tragic circumstances may make it necessary to add what would otherwise go without saying: Suffering does not always lead to belief either. Whoever coined the adage "There are no atheists in foxholes" probably lived far from the line of fire. There are both believers and disbelievers in foxholes, just as there are both believers and disbelievers among those who have known little sorrow and hardship. Our experience of the vicissitudes of life may color our experience of belief or doubt, but growth in belief or doubt is not dependent on such circumstances.

Belief by Example

Some have suggested that belief is acquired from a different aspect of our environment, not from the amount of suffering or happiness we experience, but from those believing people with whom we have associated. It is suggested that belief is taught by example. Sometimes it seems as if belief is not taught but "caught." Perhaps belief is like some kind of beneficent disease, and the way to educate people in belief is to expose them repeatedly to people who already believe. In this view the church is a community of people that can serve as a kind of quarantine in reverse: It is within the church, in a community of people who believe, that a person is most likely to "catch" belief. One respected Christian educator, John Westerhoff III, boldly asserts this: "Our children will have faith if we have faith and are faithful." [5]

There is an element of truth in this, of course, but is it really that simple? To be sure, those who believe in God can often point to those whom they credit with having influenced them through the example of their belief. There is some truth in the assertion that being exposed to people who believe can be very important in our own spiritual development. But the theory that belief is the result of such exposure does not explain the different responses among those who are exposed to the same examples. Why is it that among children raised in the same family, exposed to the same examples of belief, some will grow up with belief and others will not? Why is it that when people serve and worship within the same community of belief, the same church, some will find their belief deepened and others will not? And how can it be that some were exposed to what is perhaps the greatest example of belief, the belief of Jesus, and yet never "caught" his belief? There is a mystery about the whole process that is not adequately explained by the assertion that belief is learned by example. It is as if several pans of dough were put in the same oven to bake for the same period of time and yet some come out risen, warm and golden brown loaves of bread while other remain pale dough. It is as if two people went out in the same driving rain, each without an umbrella, but one comes back dripping and the other comes back as dry as the desert wind. Being exposed to examples of belief and associating with a faith community can certainly be of help to those who seek to believe in ways that we will consider in a subsequent chapter. But for now we must grant that belief is not "caught" by any sure or dependable means.

We return again to the question, why do some believe in God and other do not? To ask much the same question in a more directly personal way: Is there anything we can do to find belief or increase the belief we may already have?

Belief as Will

It is sometimes asserted that belief is not something that we discover through instruction, experience, or example but is instead a matter of will. According to this view we choose between the two options of belief and disbelief. We may consider all the evidence but eventually we must decide whether to believe or doubt. There is real appeal in this understanding. It would explain why people who have been given the same instruction, have experienced roughly the same proportions of hardship and happiness, and have been exposed to the same examples of belief can still draw very different conclusions about the existence of God. After all, people are not like pans of dough, which are given no choice as to whether they will rise or not. We have wills. We can choose to respond to influences in individual ways. We can choose to rise to belief or not.

For all its appeal there are still problems with reducing belief to a matter of will. William James advocated the determinative role of will in his famous address "The Will to Believe." Yet even in the midst of his eloquent presentation, James himself points to one unresolved issue. Belief may be a matter of will, but we cannot will to believe just anything. He writes,

> Can we, by any effort of our will, or by any strength of wish that it were true, believe ourselves well and about when we are roaring with rheumatism in bed, or feel certain that the sum of the two one-dollar bills in our pocket must be a hundred dollars? We can say any of these things, but we are absolutely impotent to believe them. [6]

So James grants that for us to will to believe something, it must first be a living option for us. The proposition must first seem a real possibility and have considerable allure and attraction for us before we can will to believe it.

At first it may seem as if we can eliminate the mystery of why some believe while others do not by attributing the difference to a matter of will. Perhaps unfortunately, this proves not to be so. Attributing belief to the will merely pushes the mystery to an earlier point because it does not explain why some propositions are "living options" for some and not for others. Why do some find the concept of the Christian God of sufficient plausibility and others do not? Those who assert that belief is an exercise of the will cannot fully answer such a question.

Besides this difficulty, even though we may accept in principle that people believe because they have decided to believe, we need to add that we do not usually experience belief as we do other things we decide by our will. When we decide to marry a certain person or decide to become a sausage maker instead of a carpenter, we are aware at the time that we are making a decision. But belief in God is usually not experienced in this way. If it is a decision it is a strange decision indeed because we are not aware of making it. When people of belief relate their own experience, they do not speak of willing their belief. Rather they relate that they simply found themselves believing, not because of their effort to assert their will and sometimes in spite of those efforts. They gain their belief through a process that they themselves do not fully understand.

We need to consider one final objection to the notion that belief is a matter of will. If the difference between those who believe and those who doubt is a matter of will, that merely adds insult to injury for those who long to believe in God, but find that belief elusive. Such a theory says, "Not only are you to go without the belief you long for, but it's your own damned fault (quite literally!)." When, in Lewis Carroll's *Through the*

Looking Glass, Alice confessed that she could not believe the White Queen's assertions that she was "just one hundred and one, five months, and a day," the Queen replied in exasperation, "Try again: draw a long breath, and shut your eyes."[7] Of course, the Queen's advice may sound absurd, but at least Alice could easily dismiss the queen's claims because very little was at stake in whether or not she believed those claims. But when we are considering a matter of such significance as finding belief in God, a belief with implications that range farther that the eye can see, a belief for which we may yearn more than anything else in our experience, the advice simply to try again and try harder this time is more than absurd; it is downright cruel. A role for the will is discussed in chapter 6, but it can be concluded at this point that it is not sufficient, or entirely fair, to contend that belief is simply a matter of asserting will.

Belief as a Gift

Much of this chapter has been spent in considering and then dismissing various explanations of why some people believe while others do not. If we cannot be taught to believe, if belief is not necessarily dependent on our experience of suffering and happiness, if belief is not something that can always be "caught" by example, and if it is not a matter of will, what remains for us?

Perhaps now we may be able to appreciate the statements by the author of Ephesians that faith is not an achievement of any kind but a gift from God. "By grace you have been saved through faith; and this is not your own doing, it is the gift of God" (Ephesians 2:8). There are two radical assertions in this one statement. The first is that contrary to the traditional Hebrew understanding, our relationship with God is not dependent on our fulfillment of the law, but instead we are brought into proper relationship with God through faith. The writer of Ephesians then takes a second giant step: Our faith is not another kind of human achievement. We do not receive belief because of our efforts; sometimes we receive it in spite of those efforts. It is a gift.

By definition, a gift is something we are powerless to give ourselves. We do not have the power to earn a gift by any means. For a gift to be a gift it must be given by someone else. But where does this understanding leave the person who does not believe but longs to believe? And where does it leave the person who may believe in some measure but longs to believe more fully? Is there nothing such a person can do?

We may not be able to give ourselves the gift of belief, but that does not mean we are utterly without options. Those who would be recipients of such a gift can learn to recognize the gift when it is offered. Also we can learn the many and varied ways of keeping our hands open to receive the gift rather than reject it.

To be sure, in the lives of some the gift of belief is presented with such power that the one to whom it is presented could hardly keep from recognizing it, would no more think of rejecting it than he or she would toss away life itself. But for others it is not that simple. The gift of belief is most often given in less dramatic ways, perhaps in a package that is not clearly marked and so is never recognized. For others, receiving the gift poses difficulties as well as blessings, for it is unlike other gifts in that we are not always sure when we have it or how we can keep it. And on occasion just when we are ready to reach out to receive the gift of belief, it can seem to be yanked out of our reach as if pulled by a string. At such times it can seem more like a practical joke than a gift.

Belief in God, then, is a gift from God. We cannot learn belief or will belief, but that does not mean that we are utterly helpless. We can learn how to keep our eyes open to recognize the gift of belief when it is presented. And we can learn how to keep our hands open to receive this gift when it is offered. God may be the gracious giver of belief, but we must be the gracious recipients of that gift if it is to have meaning and power.

The remaining chapters of this book will examine just how we can do these things, but first consideration must be given to another kind of gift entirely.

Questions for Reflection

- Have you ever heard someone offer some kind of "proof" for the existence of God? Did you find it persuasive or helpful?

- Have you found doubt arising out of your own experience of hardship or tragedy?

- Have you ever tried to believe something?

- Do you experience belief as a gift? If so, as a gift from whom?

CHAPTER TWO

The Important Role of Doubt

W<small>E HAVE SEEN THAT BELIEF</small> in God is a gift. Now we can move on to consider the still more difficult truth: Doubt is also a gift.

Belief is a gift in that it cannot be earned. Certainly we cannot give it to ourselves. Belief can be received only from another. But belief also *feels* like a gift. It is received as other gifts are, with eagerness and gratitude. If belief were presented to us wrapped as a gift, we would tear off the wrapping paper with the zest of a child who is finally allowed to open the package that contains his or her heart's desire.

We think of gifts as welcome, even fun, so it is difficult to think of doubt as a gift. Belief is the gift, we think, while doubt seems like the experience of one for whom the gift seems never to arrive. If we could bring ourselves to consider that doubt may also be a gift given to us by God, it would seem at first a strange gift indeed. It is a gift we would not ask for, and, receiving it, we would scarcely thank the giver. If the gift of doubt were wrapped, we would choose to leave it unopened. To be sure, we can no more give ourselves doubt than we can give ourselves belief. But in the case of doubt, this fact seems strangely moot because who would choose to give oneself doubt? Doubt seems more like a curse than a gift and hardly like a gift from a gracious God.

Because the experience of doubt is seldom received as welcome, it is difficult for us to understand doubt as a gift. Doubt confers special blessings, but they are hard blessings. Doubt may not satisfy our heart's desire, but doubt can be the kind of gift that uniquely satisfies our heart's need. That need for doubt may be too deep to recognize, too difficult to desire.

So this chapter is written in praise of doubt. To be sure, doubt is not usually treated to paeans of appreciation. Doubt is more often viewed as the disreputable party crasher than it is toasted as the guest of honor. Therefore, words of praise may be surprising; most people who pick up a book like this want to bury doubt, not praise it.

Not all expressions of doubts are worthy of praise. The more invidious forms of doubt will be considered elsewhere. For now it is enough to consider that doubt can play an important role in our lives and that doubt can even be the servant of faith. By receiving doubt as a gift, by recognizing our need for doubt as well as confronting its difficulties, we can be better prepared to live a life of faith. Indeed, it may be only after we have received God's Gift of doubt that we will be prepared to receive God' greater gift of belief.

Doubt and Growth

We can begin to appreciate the important role of doubt by recognizing the ways in which it can create the possibility for growth. As Galileo once asserted, "Doubt is the father of discovery." This is true in every human endeavor. If Columbus had never experienced doubt, he never would have discovered the new world. After all, the accepted view in Columbus's day was that the world is flat. Columbus had to entertain considerable doubt about that view before he could ever undertake such a voyage. At the time in which this country was founded, the accepted wisdom of the civilized world was that the general populace was not wise enough for self-governance. The framers of the Constitution had to doubt that wisdom in order to set out on the voyage of great discovery that we call democracy.

Then too, it was important for those of another generation to doubt even these doubters, for someone had to doubt the wisdom represented in the Constitution for women and blacks to win the right to vote.

Doubt plays an equally important role in religious growth and discovery. Without religious doubt, we would be seduced by the first easy faith that came our way. What would happen if we never doubted the beliefs of our childhood? Whatever beliefs first occupied our minds would take up permanent residence. I would still think of my parents as all-powerful and myself as immortal. I would still believe that my family could take me to the Land of Oz on the next family vacation. I would still picture God living behind a cloud, picnicking with my deceased grandparents and getting crumbs in his beard. Somewhere along the line I had to doubt all of these ideas to make room for other beliefs.

Tom Sawyer believed that if he planted five marbles in the ground under a full moon and mumbled certain secret words, the marbles would reproduce and multiply. He believed that for many years, until one night he put it to a test. The marbles were planted, the moon was full, the magic words were spoken, and—nothing happened. Mark Twain says that at that moment the foundation of Tom's faith was shaken. But there is another way of viewing it: From that time on Tom stopped believing in just anything that came along. Through doubt he began to grow.

Jesus did say that unless we become like children we will never enter the "kingdom of heaven." Perhaps no other passage of scripture has been the victim of so many sentimental—and misleading—interpretations. According to such interpretations, Jesus praises children for their wide-eyed trust and simple belief, for their complete freedom from doubt. What needs to be noted is that at every other point Jesus encourages his listeners to grow into new understandings of God's ways and expectations. When we set Jesus' words of praise for children in the context of his other teachings, it becomes clear that he was not encouraging hearers to remain children in their beliefs. Rather he was encouraging them to be childlike, this is, eager to grow up. (Have you ever known a child who was not eager to grow up?) He was praising the child's teachable spirit, a mind that is open to new truth and a heart that is open to new loyalties. A child is not free from questions. Quite the opposite. To be like a child is to have a mouth full of questions that pour out in unpredictable, even embarrassing ways: "If you can't see or hear God, how can you be sure God is there?" "If we are all made in the image of God, why are some of us ugly?" Or that big question that is found in the smallest of words, "Why?"

When Jesus says that children will be first in the kingdom of heaven, we can be sure that if the trip to the kingdom is like any other trip in the company of a child, there will be many questions asked along the way. Though the questions are incessant, and often difficult, they do not impede the journey to the kingdom. They actually advance it. Such questions can clear away old conceptions so that new understandings of God can grow.

To be sure, such questions cannot yet be called doubt, because as children we have a virtually unlimited ability to believe what we are told. Initially we accept the answers to our questions. Reliance on authority is our only access to truth because we have no independent knowledge of our own. Because for a child everything that is heard is accepted as true, a child's belief will be a jumble of truth and fantasy. Descriptions of heaven mix with pictures of Oz. The reality of God is accepted in the same way as is the existence of Santa Claus. In fact, the two can keep such close company in the mind of a child that they begin to look alike: God becomes an elderly man with a beard who gives gifts to good children. Heaven and Oz, God and Santa Claus, life after death and enchanted forests—as a child we received them all in such trust and such confusion.

When a child presses questions like a badgering trial lawyer, eventually the answers received do not satisfy, or, as with Tom Sawyer, they do not correspond with direct experience. It is then that doubt has an opportunity. It is only after we have developed this capacity to doubt that we can begin to sort out a child's grab bag of motley beliefs.

When we are old enough to have the first stirrings of doubt about what we are told, the experience can be very disturbing. Having opened up the possibility for doubt, we wonder where the reach of doubt may end. Having once accepted these realities wholesale, we then wonder if they must now be rejected wholesale. When, under my searching cross-examination, my parents finally, reluctantly conceded that there is no such person as Santa Claus, I first mourned the loss of the jolly old elf. But very shortly the focus of my concern became the continued reality of those other beliefs that had occupied the same place in my heart and mind that Santa Claus did. And so I quickly asked my parents, "What else is not true?" When even Santa Claus can be dismissed so summarily, who is next? Once one closely held belief is called into question, other beliefs are threatened.

This is true not only in the mind of a child. It is true whenever a belief is called into question. When Copernicus demonstrated that, contrary to popular assumption, the earth revolves around the sun, it caused shock waves of doubt in virtually every area of human belief and knowledge. If the sun does not revolve around the earth how can we be sure that other things we believe are still true? Can we still believe there is a God? Likewise, when Darwin challenged the historical accuracy of the scriptural assertion that God created the world in six days, the whole scriptural authority was called into question. If we cannot trust the Bible on this point, how can we believe any of it?

Whether it is a child coming to terms with the new understanding that there is no Santa Claus or a whole civilization coming to terms with the revolutionary discoveries of Copernicus or Darwin, doubt about one point of belief is threatening because it can call into questions every other belief. And so the appearance of doubt can give rise to great fear. This is especially true in religious matters, where so much is at stake. In religious matters the fear occasioned by doubt is that one might discover that one's whole life has been built on a foundation that does not exist.

If people are generally afraid to entertain religious doubts, they may still respond to that fear in quite different ways. When some people first experience doubt they respond by rejecting all belief. If some of what they believed about God turns out not to be true, they conclude that there is no God. Having abstained from doubt so completely, they now go on a binge of doubt. Lewis Carroll offered this advice to a young friend who had gone through just such a transition: "Don't be in such a hurry to believe next time—I'll tell you why—if you set to work to believe everything, you will tire the muscles of your mind, and then you'll be so weak you won't be able to believe the simplest true things."[1]

Others respond to the first appearance of doubt in different ways. They close ranks around certain of their beliefs and simply refuse to entertain doubts about them. No further inquiry is allowed. No new understanding will move them. Anything that may prove contrary to their hardened belief is either refuted or simply dismissed. As different as the confirmed atheist and the rigidly dogmatic believer may appear at first, they are both seeking ways to escape doubt. Both are fearful responses to the presence of doubt.

Often it takes courage to doubt. It takes courage to reexamine those beliefs we had assumed were beyond the reach of doubt. If people do not have the courage to doubt, any new knowledge or experience poses a threat. Lacking the courage to doubt, people will protect their hardened beliefs against new understandings with great vehemence, even violence. For instance, it was those who could not doubt their firmly held religious convictions who crucified Jesus. If this son of a carpenter who talks of God in the untutored accent of his backwater hometown is actually God's Chosen One, then they must call into question all they had firmly held about God's ways. By contrast, it was only those who could doubt their ideas and cherished traditions about how God would act in the world who were prepared to receive Jesus as the promised Messiah.

Doubt as the Guardian of Faith

Doubt can be the servant of faith, guarding us from inadequate ideas of God. In his classic book *Your God Is Too Small,* J. B. Phillips describes thirteen such simplistic images of God that are commonly held.[2] They range from "Resident Policeman" to "Heavenly Bosom." Many of these immature images of God are formed in childhood and are carried frozen and stiff into adulthood because creative doubts about them were never entertained. If these beliefs are held unexamined they can stunt our spiritual growth, preventing us from claiming a deep and mature faith. The challenge implicit in Phillip's book is this: "If you have the same concept of God you had when you were a child, or even ten years ago, your God is too small." Without doubt our beliefs can be little more than a collection of sanctified stupidity. Our image of God needs to be stretched if our relationship with God is to grow. And that is possible only through doubt. Doubt can keep us from surrendering to any fad or fanaticism that comes along. It is through doubt that God can be delivered from our too small, puny definitions of God's majesty and mystery and power.

Sometimes when people question the existence of God, they are actually questioning the existence of a God who is inadequately imagined. When people say to me that they do not believe in God, I usually ask, "What is the God you do not believe in?" Often the God that is described is small and simplistic. They don't believe in a God who is like a kindly grandfather. Or, by contrast, they don't believe in a God who is a cruel snatcher of souls, visiting death upon children because he wants them with him in heaven. To such depictions of God I can only respond, "I don't believe in that God either." In some, agnosticism is simply the refusal to accept such inadequate concepts of God. By rejecting such images of God the agnostic may actually be closer to the truth than the naïve believer. As Tennyson's *In Memoriam* affirmed: "There lives more faith in honest doubt, believe me, than in half the creeds."

It is important for both believer and agnostic to free God from such inadequate images. A believer must understand that God is not captured in such childish understandings in order to claim more mature faith. An agnostic needs to separate God from images of God that are too small in order to experience any belief at all. For both believer and agnostic, doubt can play a crucial creative role.

It is necessary to entertain doubt not only so that we might discard childish beliefs and inadequate concepts of God. It can also be important to doubt those understandings of God that turn out to be worthy of our continued allegiance. It is through doubt that we can reject falsehood. Conversely, through doubt, truth itself may need to be discarded so that it can be received again as truth. In this way doubt can help us move from secondhand faith to a firsthand faith.

As young children, our receptivity to the beliefs of our parents and others is as complete as that of the French peasant who asked Louis XI, "Sire, what are our opinions?" When we are young children our thought is as imitative as our speech. We can get by with this kind of secondhand faith when we are young. For a developing mind, however, that is not enough. Former certainties are called in question. The whole range of received understandings and values is examined, including religious beliefs. When a child is young, religious beliefs are accepted because they are held by the parents. But when the child becomes a young adult the opposite may happen: Those same religious beliefs may be rejected because they are held by the same parents. This change in attitude reveals something more profound than the mere contrariness of youth. Rather, for beliefs to be truly our own, it is often necessary to disengage from our inherited beliefs in order that, at a different stage, we may come to believe again, but with a big difference. The beliefs are now our own. They are not someone else's hand-me-downs. Goethe put it this way: "What you have inherited from your fathers you must earn for yourself before you can call it your own." If we become free to doubt what we are told, we then become free to have our very own belief in God, a firsthand belief that is real and personal. That is why Thoreau expressed his need for doubt almost defiantly: "If I could not doubt, I should not believe."

We can do more than grudgingly admit that a period of doubt is an unfortunate but predictable part of growing up, much as adolescent acne is. Instead, we should recognize that doubt can play a positive role in faith development. A time of deep doubt can be as important as activating the clutch of a car: It allows us to make the crucial shift from a secondhand belief to a firsthand belief. If we are interested in the religious development of a young person, we may be concerned when that young person is in a period of serious and thoroughgoing religious doubt, but there may be greater cause for concern if he or she never experiences any such doubt. That is why, when a bishop of another era asked a young candidate for ordination, "Have you ever had any difficulties in religion?" and the candidate replied without hesitation, "None, sir," the bishop could only respond, "I am so sorry." The absence of doubt can indicate that a person is frozen in his or her faith development. Such a person's faith can be like thin soup, not nourishing enough or the long haul.

To say that doubt can play an important role in the life of faith, that it can help us move beyond childish beliefs and claim a firsthand belief in God, is not to imply that the experience of doubt is easy to endure. Frederick Buechner defines doubt as "the ants in the pants of faith. They keep it alive and moving."[3] As frivolous as this definition may seem, it reminds us that the experience of doubt is seldom greeted as welcome. Doubt is uncomfortable. But then, those things that allow for growth are seldom easy. For instance, whoever promised that adolescence would be easy? Adolescence is difficult precisely because it is a period of dramatic physical and psychological development. We can expect that our spiritual adolescence, at whatever age we experience it, will be no less difficult.

It is difficult to pull up anchor and set out for uncharted waters. Our underdeveloped ideas of God and our immature relationship with God may not satisfy, but they have the advantage of familiarity. Sometimes familiarity breeds contentment. We may, in retrospect, declare that growth was necessary and worth the pain it caused, but at the time the possibility for growth is presented to us we may see only what we must give up in the process. In George Bernard Shaw's play

Major Barbara, Undershaft says, "You have learned something. That always feels, at first, as if you had lost something." Doubt simultaneously extends a promise and poses a threat. It is the promise of what may lie ahead. It is the threat of what must be left behind. Such a promise and such a threat always accompany growth. The growth we can experience through doubt is no exception.

Tenacity of Doubt

When we speak of doubt as necessary for growth, we should not imagine that doubt is something that we can merely grow out of in the way we eventually grow out of the awkwardness of adolescence. Indeed, if growth in faith is a task worthy of a lifetime, we cannot ever expect to be totally free from doubt.

The towering examples of believers within the Christian tradition were not people who were free from doubt, even in their maturity. After all, belief and doubt are not found in isolation within human lives, even in the lives of the saints. Tertullian, a leading figure in the early church who devoted himself to the study of scriptures and the cause of Christ, is also remembered for his dictum, "I believe because it is impossible." Augustine, whose theological reflections became a foundation for Christian thought in every subsequent generation and whose *Confessions* is still a prototype for spiritual autobiography, also prayed, "O Lord, I would have turned to thee, but I had neither the power nor the will, for every time I thought of God nothing real or substantial was presented to my mind." Thomas Aquinas, whose monumental *Summa Theologica* was the first and remains the most influential systematic exposition of the Christian faith, confessed, "The most man can know is that he does not know God." Examples can be added, indeed multiplied, from every generation.

We may be tempted to extract some rather meager lessons from the striking presence of doubt in the lives of these great believers. We might conclude that no one is perfect. Or we might cite them as evidence that belief is simply too difficult to sustain. But something more seems to be at work here. We sometimes speak of doubt and belief as opposites, but perhaps it is more accurate to think of doubt as a shadow cast by belief. After all, the very doubts held by these people of belief attest to the scale and power of what they believed. Their doubt actually gave God a backhanded compliment: God is too mighty, too grand and mysterious to be fully grasped. The saying, "If you are not confused you do not understand the situation," in reference to God might be rendered, "If you do not doubt, you do not understand God." Augustine himself gives testimony to this: "God is not what you imagine or what you think you understand. For if you understand, you have failed."

A God who is worthy of belief is also subject to doubt. After all, the only things we do not doubt are things like 2 + 2 = 4. But who would worship a 2 + 2 = 4 kind of God? A god who could be so easily understood would lack the complexities and nuances of personality. Such a God would not move in mysterious ways. Such a God would be predictable, easy to understand. And if God were that predictable, that easy to understand, we might eliminate doubt, but we would also eliminate the grandeur and majesty of God. Flannery O'Connor wrote to a friend who was struggling to believe, "Whatever you do anyway, remember these things are mysteries and that if they were such that we could understand them, they wouldn't be worth understanding. A god you could understand would be less than yourself."[4]

Trying to make God more accessible to human understanding always ends up in idolatry. In biblical times the idolater's God might be represented in gold or wood. This God could be imagined and defined, captured and secure, a God that did not need to be doubted because it could be seen and touched, a changeless God and a lifeless God. More modern images of God also can be reduced to that which is less subject to doubt. God can be understood as simply the refinement and elevation of the most noble human impulses. God can be pictured as the impersonal force of life in the universe. Whether it is the ancient worshiper dancing around a statue or the enlightened modern believer rallying around an image of God that is easily captured in words, the result is the same: When we set out to create images of God that are accessible, easily grasped, such images end up being merely images of ourselves writ large, yet less than ourselves because there is no life left in them. Such "gods" may not be hard to believe, but that is precisely the problem. They are not subject to our doubt because they are not worthy of our belief. Some people do not doubt because they simply do not believe very much.

That is why, by contrast, the biblical descriptions of God are really nondescriptions. They remind us that God never sat for a portrait. They affirm God's freedom and majesty by insisting that God cannot be captured in a graven image or even described in words.

The larger realities and deeper mysteries of God are those that are open to doubt, but they are also large enough and deep enough to show God to us. One's doubt does not necessarily recede as one's belief increases, and certainly not in any direct correlation. Rather, to reach for great belief is to risk great doubt. It should be little surprise, then, that those people of most profound belief are the same people who are subject to great doubt. We should expect that the valleys seem deepest to those who have been to the mountaintop.

We may want to pray that God remove all doubt from us, but we also can be grateful when such prayers seem to go unanswered. The only way to make the human experience of

God less subject to doubt is to reduce God to a more accessible scale. In other words, the only way to eliminate all doubt is to make of God something that is unworthy of belief. We can be thankful that when we reach for God we are stretching toward a reality of such magnitude and power that we open ourselves to the presence of doubts. Only a God who is too mighty to be encompassed by certainty, too wonderful to be found only within the borders of our imaginations, is worthy of belief.

Doubt, like belief, is a gift. Though we may not receive the gift of doubt with the same sense of appreciation as we do the gift of belief, it meets needs that are deeper than we can usually recognize. It is through doubt that we can move beyond childish understandings of God. It is through doubt that we can move from hearsay belief to a firsthand experience of God. And it is through doubt that we can continually confront God's mystery and majesty. If the gift of faith were wrapped, we would open it eagerly. If the gift of doubt we wrapped, we might choose to leave it unopened. But such a choice is not offered to us. In the end, we discover that both gifts are in the same package.

Questions for Reflection

- Have you ever experienced doubt as a gift? In what way?

- Did you, at some point in your life, have images of God that later seemed "too small"?

- What do you make of the observation that, through history, many towering examples of believers also experienced great doubt?

CHAPTER THREE

The Differences Between Belief and Faith

THE DIFFERENCES BETWEEN BELIEF AND FAITH are seldom recognized. We often use the words interchangeably, and, of course, they have much in common. But they are not entirely synonymous, and the differences are critical. When we consider the differences between belief and faith, we are not tinkering with dry intellectual distinctions. Rather, we are dealing with central issues that have far-reaching implications. Understanding the differences between faith and belief is not only important in itself; being clear about the differences is vital to our understanding of the nature of doubt and the role doubt plays in the life of faith.

Belief and Intellect, Faith and the Whole Person

One major difference between belief and faith can be stated quite simply: Belief is an act of intellect, whereas faith is an act of the whole person. When someone asks, "Do you believe in God?" we usually take that question to mean, "Do you think there is a God? Are you of the conviction that God exists?" When the question "Do you believe in God?" is asked within a Christian context, we further assume that we are being asked if we believe in the existence of the kind of God who is described in the Bible or worshiped by the church. Whatever the context, however, the question is largely an intellectual one: Do you think there is a God? Or do you think there is a God like the one described by the Christian tradition? When you take stock of the world, with it mysteries and miseries, does it make sense to say that there is such a God?

"Faith," on the other hand, is a much richer word. When we say we have faith in God, it implies that we do something more than conclude that there is a God or a God of a particular description. It is like the instance when I say of another human being, "I have faith in her," I mean many things, including "I trust her, I rely on her, I love her, I depend on her." To have faith in God, then, implies a whole range of ways one actively relates to God. Faith requires much more than a mere intellectual assent to the statement that a God exists or the mere conviction that God has certain qualities. Rather, faith is a living, dynamic relationship that is more akin to trust than anything else. We may *believe* that God has "the whole world in his hands," but *faith* is the act of trust by which we put ourselves in God's hands.

Passive Belief, Active Faith

There is another way to state the difference. We can sit back and believe, but we cannot sit back and have faith. We can sit back in dry, calculating, measured belief, scratch our chins and say, "Yes, I believe there is a God," and leave it at that. We might even go so far as to say, "I believe there is a loving God" and still not have that belief change the way we live our lives. It may strike us as strange that someone could come to believe in the existence of a God, even a God who cares, without that belief prompting any further action, but that is just the kind of strange responses we often witness. Such armchair belief is common and relativity easy; it can have as few implications for the way we live our lives as the belief that water is one part oxygen and two parts hydrogen. Such a belief can leave us where we are, unmoved and undisturbed.

The writer of the letter of James was referring to such believers without faith when he wrote, "You believe that God is one; you do well. Even the demons believe—and shudder. Do you want to be shown, you senseless person, that faith apart from works is barren?" (James 2:19-20). Pure intellectual acceptance that there is a God, and even acceptance that there is one God, though it surely must be considered a component in the life of faith, is not worth very much in itself. There is no small amount of sarcasm in the words, "You do well. Even the demons believe—and shudder." James, like the other New Testament writers, takes it for granted that even a fool or a demon cannot fail to believe in some kind of God. But if nothing in the way of action or relationship flows from that belief, it is worthless.

If, on the other hand, we have faith in God, that is something different. To believe in God all we need say is, "True," but to have faith in God we must go on to say, "Yes."

Let us imagine we are at a circus. A skilled high-wire artist has accompanied so many marvelous feats that the audience has come to believe he can do almost anything. The ringmaster addresses the crowd: "Ladies and gentlemen, how many of you believe that this daring man can ride safely over the high wire on his bicycle while carrying someone on his shoulders? If you believe he can do it, please raise your hand!" If we were in the audience, we might raise our hand along with all the others, a great, silent chorus of belief. "Very well, then," says the ringmaster, seeing the almost unanimous vote of confidence, "now who would like to be the first to volunteer to sit on his shoulders?"

The difference between belief and faith is the difference between staying in our seat and volunteering to climb on the shoulders of the high-wire artist. Faith is not passive or merely intellectual. Faith does not let us sit back with comfortable detachment. Faith gets us out of our seats, and what we do by faith is actively to put our trust in God.

It may be surprising to the modern reader of the Bible that Jesus offered no arguments for the existence of God. The reason is that the people Jesus encountered did not lack a belief in God. What many of them lacked, however, was the kind of living, trusting relationship with God that properly can be called faith. John Baillie reflected on this aspect of Jesus' teaching:

> Those whom He rebuked for their lack of faith were not men who denied God with the top of their minds, but men who, while apparently incapable of doubting Him with the top of their minds, *lived* as though he did not exist. So far as our records show, He never had to deal with the kind of men to whom He would have to say, "You think you do not believe in God, yet in the bottom of your hearts you know that you are surrounded by His holiness and love." Rather He had to deal with men to whom He had to say, "You think you *do* believe in God, yet you refuse to trust Him in every hour and circumstance of need."[1]

Jesus was consistently critical of those whose religious life was long on belief but short on faith. The most frequent objects of His ire were the learned religious leaders who seemed to lack a living relationship with the One about whom they had learned so much. This is not uncommon: Those who define God best can be the very ones who understand God least. As Pascal observed, "The knowledge of God is very far from the love of Him."[2] It may be common for those who know so much about God to lack a living relationship with God, but it is an absurd spectacle, as absurd as would be the behavior of people who love to read cookbooks and memorize recipes and yet themselves never eat anything.

Belief versus Trust

It is not belief in certain ideas about God, but trust in the person of God that is central to the gospel. One story in the Gospel of Mark illustrates this concern, even if we leave aside the question of whether or not it records a historical incident. As the story has it, Jesus was with the disciples in a small boat bobbing about on the Sea of Galilee during a storm. One disciple grabs the mast while another clutches the side of the boat and turns various shades of green. It is quite a storm all right, to the disciples at least, many of whom were landlubbers, uninitiated in seafaring ways. Jesus, however, is able to sleep through it all, his head on a pillow. Even the shouting wind does not awaken Jesus until a disciples asks, "Teacher, do you not care if we perish?" Then, according to the gospel account, Jesus awakes, calms the sea with a word, and turns to the disciples: "Why are you afraid? Have you no faith?" It is obvious that Jesus was not concerned with the disciples' belief in theological propositions. He was not asking the disciples to recite a creed. He was not taking this opportunity to ask them for a learned dissertation about the nature of God. Rather, what he found lacking in the disciples was faithful trust (Mark 4:35–41).

Even when Jesus asked his hearers to consider the lilies of the field, he was not—as has sometimes been supposed—using the mysterious and beautiful design of nature as evidence for the existence of God. Even if such evidence were irrefutable, as no such evidence ever is, it would only lead to a kind of belief in the existence of God that profits little. Instead, Jesus was referring to the way God cares for even the smallest parts of God's creation in order to prompt us to put more trust in God's love. He is posing a rhetorical question: If God cares so magnificently for the creatures that seem most insignificant, is it not obvious that those who are God's very children can entrust themselves to that care through faith? Once again, it is faith, and not belief, that is the object of Jesus' concern.

Of course, if we are to put ourselves in God's care through faith, it helps to believe that God exists or that God has certain qualities. Even if there is such a thing as belief without faith, no faith can be sustained without a measure of belief. We might even be tempted to say that belief is a prerequisite of faith: *If* we believe in God, *then* we can move on to putting our faith in God. But we must be careful here. Although any religious life with integrity has an intellectual component, the intellect seldom leads. This is why philosophical proofs of the existence of God seldom satisfy. God is not discovered at the end of an argument. If we divide our understandings into those that come to us through our intellect and those that come to us by another means, through what has come to be called our "heart," in religious matters the heart almost always leads. It is the heart that gives the surest conviction of God's existence and God's nature. More important, it is the heart that gives itself in trust to God. Harry Emerson Fosdick put it pointedly: "There is many a kingdom of heaven you do not get into head first."[3]

Christians are often inclined to feel apologetic about the primacy of the heart in religious matters, for the world at large has come to value understandings of the intellect more than what seem like the groundless convictions of the heart. And yet for all the value we place on reason, we follow the intuition of our heart and trust its promptings in many aspects of our lives. Pascal's words have the character of a reminder because they echo our experience: "We know the truth, not only by the reason, but also by the heart." He adds, "The heart has its reasons, which reason does not know. We feel this in a thousand things."[4] There is another way to put this: We know through reason that there are instances when reason is not enough. We know that we follow the heart's lead in some of our most fundamental relationships and convictions. We do not, for example, reason our way into love, or out of love, though we may try. But that does not mean that love is a simple whim. We do not reason our way into the surest sense of right and wrong in issues of morality. But that does not mean we should ignore our heartfelt convictions about right and wrong.

Those who expect reason to lead them to God will find themselves in the company of an unqualified guide. In fact, those who try to reason their way into a belief in the existence of God may have the experience of finding belief more and more elusive as they proceed. Such belief tends to fade, and sometimes disappear, the more closely they examine it.

Again, we are tempted to feel apologetic about this. But the elusive quality of belief under the light of pure reason is not unlike our experience in other areas of our lives. For example, it would not be difficult to find broad agreement that love is the foundation of a happy marriage. We might further agree that it is important to establish that love is present before any marriage is performed. So in the course of the wedding ceremony, the minister inserts a question to be asked of the bride and bridegroom. The question asked of the bride is, "Do you love this man?" Fair enough, and easily enough answered: "Yes, I do." Then imagine that the officiating minister follows that question with another: "Are you *sure* that you love him?" The answer comes after a moment: "Yes, yes, I am sure." And again: "Are you *absolutely certain* that you love this man?" The bride tries in vain to remain composed: "Why, yes, yes, I feel quite certain of it." And then there is one final question: "How do you know you love this man?"

How many couples would be married today if their love had been subjected to this kind of agonizing scrutiny? In the face of such questions, even a mature and living love can seem to almost disappear. Such a bride might be left with simply blurting out, "Well, I always thought I loved him." Unless, of course, she was familiar with Pascal, in which case she could say, "The heart has its reasons which reason does not know."

So it is with belief. If we wait for a firm intellectual belief in the existence of God before we act in faith, if we wait until we can affirm all that is said about God before we entrust ourselves to God's care, that time seems never to come. Belief, like love, is not given a chance to grow when it is watched so carefully. Imagine a man picking up a woman at her home for a first date and from the first moment of that first date asking himself, "Am I in love with this person?" They eat dinner. He wonders, "Am I in love?" They go dancing. He asks himself, "Am I in love?" They walk home and talk, and all the while he interrogates his own heart in silence: "Is this love?" It is hard to imagine a circumstance less conducive to the growth of love. Such scrutiny does not give love a chance. It is the same with belief in God. It is difficult for belief to grow while it is being watched. Those who try to acquire belief through concentration and effort will likely find belief ever more difficult, in much the same way as the insomniac who is always asking, "Is this sleep? Am I drifting off to sleep now?" will find sleep elusive.

Belief in God is not an achievement that is completed only through focused attention. In fact, it is much more likely that such belief will sneak up on us when we are not looking. Here is the twist: Belief is most likely to come when we act in a faithful manner. It is by entrusting ourselves to God that we can come to see that there is a God and that God is worthy of our trust. John Wesley put it this way: "Live by faith until you have faith." That statement reverses our expectations. We assume that we must first feel prayerful and that, if we succeed, prayer will follow. Experience, however, often reverses the order: It is by the practice of prayer that we can come to feel prayerful. We may wait in vain for a sense of worshipful reverence before

God because it is only through worship that we can come to understand that God is worthy of worship. Likewise, it is by living in a faithful manner, obeying God's commandments, learning of God, praising God, serving God's children, seeking God's help, committing ourselves to God's care, that we can come to believe in the God with whom we have been in relationship through all of these faithful activities.

Reasoned belief in God, then, is far from being a prerequisite to faith in God. This understanding has important implications. It means that we do not have to have an unshakeable belief in the affirmations that we have heard about God before we act in faith. We do not need to be certain that God even exists. It can be in living as if God exists that we can come to see that, yes, God does indeed exist. What we need before all else is not to have God explained. Instead, what we need is to experience God by entrusting ourselves to God's care. That is, a vital relationship with God must be lived through before it is thought through. It is true of faith as it is true of so much in our lives: It is more likely that we will act ourselves into a new way of thinking than think ourselves into a new way of acting.

Of course, this does not mean that the question of whether or not there is a God is a slight one, or that the question is undeserving of our attention. Rather, we cannot expect that question to be answered to our full satisfaction before we entrust ourselves to God through faith. Think of the father who seeks to have Jesus cure his epileptic son (Mark 9:14–29). When he catches up with the disciples, Jesus is still on a mountaintop. The disciples seem anxious to help as their master would have. Like children in the attic trying on their parents' clothes, they lay on hands and say a few words. But nothing happens. When Jesus arrives, he wants to know what all the commotion is about. The man has to tell the whole story of the seizures again, all the ugly details. He blurts out the story as fast as he can and does not measure every word: "If you are able to do anything, have pity on us and help us." Jesus jumps on him: "If you are able! All things can be done for the one who believes."

The man might have left right then if his son had not cried out just at that moment. Instead the man turns to Jesus. If the human mouth could say two things at once, his would have. Instead, he says two things in quick succession: "I believe; help my unbelief." The father is expressing doubt that Jesus can heal his son. He believes and does not believe, an almost universal mixture. And yet he does not wait for his doubts to be resolved before he seeks out Jesus. Indeed, he is doubting the very one he is looking to for help. Before his doubts are resolved, before he can claim any certainty about God's nature and God's power, before he can affirm without reservation that God can heal and, more to the point, that God can heal through Jesus, the father entrusts himself and his son to the care of Jesus. We are not told whether the faith in Jesus that the father expressed led to a firmer belief in God's care and healing power, and yet it is clear that he did not wait for belief before acting in faith.

People can, and often do, entrust themselves to God's care even while they are enmeshed in perplexity and uncertainty in their beliefs about God. In his latter years, Albert Schweitzer struggled with his Christian faith. He wrote that he was entertaining the most crucial doubts about the care of God, the efficacy of prayer, the divinity of Christ, the reality and purpose of the resurrection. And yet during that period, this same man, while never letting go of his doubts, affirms, "I have decided to surrender myself to that infinite being who gives my wretched life its meaning and its riches." Albert Camus was right: There are times when we must make a 100 percent commitment to something about which we are only 51 percent certain.

Belief versus Doubt, Faith versus Pride

It may be hard for us to understand how a person can entrust himself or herself to God in faith while holding doubts, because we have come to see faith and doubt as opposites. Here again, our confusion can be attributed to a case of mistaken identity. Such confusion results from a lack of clarity about the differences between belief and faith. It is belief, and not faith, that is the opposite of, or at least opposed to, doubt. Either you believe the world is round, or you doubt it. Either you believe the Yankees will win the pennant, or you doubt it. Either you believe there is a God who created the world and cares for it still, or you doubt it. To say that belief and doubt are opposites is not to say that they are never found together. To the contrary, belief and doubt keep close company. Nevertheless, they are uneasy, constant companions because belief and doubt are opposed. They pull us in opposite directions, and in most questions, we must come down on one side or the other, cast our lot with either belief or doubt. We may not be able to make up our minds, but we cannot fail to make up our lives.

Faith, however, is not the opposite of doubt. Faith in God, understood as a trust that is characteristic of a living relationship, is concerned with other matters entirely. In this context it is important to remember that the image Jesus used most often to describe God's relationship with us is the metaphor of a parent relating to a child. A child may not fully understand an earthly parent. That child may even believe some humorously distorted ideas about a parent's life, what constitutes the parent's work, how that parent relates to the world. Yet in spite of those wildly mistaken "beliefs" about the parent, the child seeks and relies on the care of the parent and responds to the parent in trust. The beliefs the child holds about the parent do not invalidate that trust. As mental concepts shift and change with the introduction of new knowledge, as inadequate beliefs about the parent are replaced with more mature beliefs, that trust abides. Through all the changes, the abiding character of a child's relationship with a parent is not belief, but trust.

If we understand faith as trust, we do not have to look far to find the opposite of faith. It is not doubt, but the lack of trust, or the conviction of self-sufficiency. This is another way of saying that the opposite of faith is pride. It is pride that prompts us to declare that we are made in our own image. It is pride that leads us to entrust ourselves to ourselves. It is the prideful assumption that we have all answers, all ability, and all power to craft a meaningful life by our own efforts. This is why Jesus could be so critical of those without faith. It is not that they held mistaken ideas about God, but that they were so full of pride that they could act as if God did not exist.

Faith as a Verb

Some of our confusion about the concept of faith can be attributed to a quirk in the English language. The English language is the only European language that does not have a verb form of the word faith. In English we cannot say, "I faith, you faith, he or she faiths."

This one small characteristic of the English language can cause a lot of confusion. Since, in English, there is no verb form for the word faith, we must choose between two options, and either option can mislead us about the nature of faith. The first option is that we can settle for "I believe." But that blurs the distinction between faith and belief, a distinction that should be retained. The second option is that we can always use faith as a noun. We can say, for instance, "I have faith." But if we do that, we have implied that faith is a possession. Consider the implications: If I say I "have" something—a pen, a nose, or whatever—that implies a certain permanence or certainty. You either have it, or you do not have it. Faith, however, is not a possession; it is a capacity, a capacity for trust that is not nearly so permanent. Our faith is stronger on some days than it is on other days. We can live out our faith in God more completely at some times more than at other times.

If faith is to be properly understood, it must be understood as a verb. Faith is something we do. Indeed, if language would allow, we would say something like this: "I faith sometimes. I wish I could faith more often. In fact, I'm working toward faithing in God in all that I do." That may be grammatically painful, but it is theologically correct. Faith is not something we have with certainty, once and for all, at all times, under all circumstances. Rather, it is something we do, sometimes more easily than others, sometimes more completely than other times. Human frailty rarely allows us more than that. We are all capable of acting faithfully, but none of us is faithful always. This is very important to remember. If faith is a noun, a thing to possess, then some of us have it, and others of us do not. But if we properly understand faith as a verb, it is something we can all look for and share in.

Let us consider the story of Peter attempting to walk on water (Matthew 14:22-33). Please note that in this context we are not asking whether the event happened as recorded, but merely considering what the story, as a story, says about the nature of faith. As the gospel account has it, the disciples are on a boat on the Sea of Galilee. Jesus has sent them along without him, but none of the disciples thought to ask how he would join them so far out on the water. They are terrified when they see his figure through the mist, walking on water. Unlike a sailor who asks permission to come on board, Peter seems to ask Jesus' permission to get out of the boat: "Lord, if it is you, command me to come to you on the water." Jesus says,

"Come." So Peter, like the one fool in the crowd who agrees to climb on the shoulders of the high-wire artist, climbs out of the boat and begins a walk of trust, a walk of faith, a walk on the water.

Peter is faithing pretty well for a while. But something overcomes him. It is fear. And as Peter, "the Rock," faiths less and less, he sinks more and more, as rocks have a tendency to do. But even then, despite his fears and doubts, Peter can still faith a little. He is able to abandon his illusions of self-sufficiency long enough to cry out, "Lord, save me!" His faith does not save him, because his faith is not constant. But he is saved, despite his fickle faith, by a Lord who is constant.

Questions for Reflection

◆ In what ways are faith and belief different and in what ways are they related?

◆ John Wesley advised, "Live by faith until you have faith." Have you ever experienced this dynamic in your own life?

◆ What are some of the implications of thinking of faith as a verb rather than as a noun?

CHAPTER FOUR

On Feeling Like a Hypocrite

A RATHER THREATENING QUESTION lingers in and around the previous chapter. It is time to bring that question squarely before us so that it can be confronted.

We have seen that belief and faith are different and that we cannot wait for a firm belief in God before acting in faith. Rather, if we are to believe, we must entrust ourselves to the God who seems elusive, at best, and whose very existence we may doubt. There is another way to put it: In many instances we must act as if we believe in God before we do, in fact, believe. It is here that we confront the important and difficult question: Is that not really the same thing as hypocrisy? Put it another way: Do we not expect our actions and beliefs to be consistent? If we act as if we believe before we believe, are we not guilty of masquerading as something we are not?

In some form or another these questions are often given voice. There are always those who are more than willing to assign the label hypocrite to those who belong to a church or attend worship. They are quick to point out the seeming disparity between the actions and beliefs of the churchgoer.

Often these critics are merely expressing the unspoken suspicions of a still more persistent and disturbing critic, the inner critic within those who act as if they believe when they know that their belief would scarcely fill a cup compared to their oceans of doubt. Many of those who attend worship suspect that they are there under false pretenses. After all, is not worship for believers, for those who have resolved their doubts, or at least for those whose belief outweighs their doubt? Even the simple act of walking through the door of a church for worship seems like a clear enough affirmation of belief. Those who hold serious doubts may then conclude that they do not belong in worship, that their very presence is a misleading statement about the strength and character of their beliefs.

Usually, the worship service itself does nothing to relieve the tension between what we seem to say by our presence and what we actually believe in our hearts and minds. Things are said during worship that we may not fully accept. Affirmations are made that seem difficult, if not impossible, to believe. And if the very act of attending a gathering where such things are said and affirmed without so much as a word of objection or qualification being voiced were not enough to make us uncomfortable, during worship we are asked to *say* some of the very things about which we hold the most doubt. Through unison prayer we address the God whom we may doubt even exists. Through song we praise the acts of God that seem implausible, at best. Through the recitation of creeds we publicly affirm things we do not hold with certainty.

The inner critic knows without needing to be told that there is often an incongruity between what a person hears, or even says, during worship and what he or she firmly believes. This seeming inconsistency between expressing belief through worship while holding grave doubts can be greatly disturbing. It leads some to avoid identification with the church entirely. It leaves others suspended in an unresolved tension between what they see themselves doing and know themselves to believe, all the while wondering if that means the label hypocrite fits them after all.

Hypocrisy has few friends, no matter what the setting. But for those who would be Christians the word "hypocrite" takes on an added chastening dimension: Jesus himself used the term "hypocrite" to describe those who make a show of piety.

The very word seemed to burn hot on his tongue. To Jesus it was a fearsome accusation, used in a way that could shoot someone down at thirty paces: "Woe unto you, hypocrites!"

Jesus said that hypocrites are those who give to the poor with fanfare, a fanfare they blow on their own horn. Hypocrites pray in public in order to be seen praying, with an eye over their shoulder to see who, besides God, might be listening. Jesus assailed those of his time who were the very picture of piety. But that was their problem. They were the *picture* of piety, a picture—in two dimensions—like the façade of a Hollywood set with nothing but a sprawling empty lot behind it.

Jesus also used a number of unflattering images to describe hypocrites. He said they are like whitewashed tombs. Outwardly, the tomb is clean and prim; inwardly it seethes with decomposing flesh. Elsewhere he compared hypocrites to dishwashers who meticulously scrub and polish the outside of a bowl and place it back on the shelf without giving a thought to the food encrusted on the inside. All this attention to appearances, while the inner life of the soul rots through a lack of attention, all of life a grand charade designed to deceive.

After hearing Jesus' stinging words about hypocrites, those who seek to believe in the Christian God return to the original question with an increased sense of urgency: Are those who act as if they believe in God before they do believe accurately described as hypocrites? Is the way Jesus used the word "hypocrite" properly applied to those who appear to be making a public statement of belief—by praying, worshiping, belonging to a church—yet all the while they hold grave private doubts?

If we are to begin to answer that question, we must consider a person's motivations. The hypocrite is motivated by the praise of others. Jesus commented on those who made a show of almsgiving and prayer by saying, "Truly I tell you, they have received their reward" (Matthew 6:2 and 6:5). It is a reward paid out in the common currency of admiration from one's fellows. The hypocrite seeks personal gain by presenting a praiseworthy face toward the world.

The picture Jesus draws of the hypocrite giving alms or praying at first seems to be the picture of a person being very public in his or her actions, confident and bold. But, in reality, such a person is actually being very private. Much is hidden. It is an incomplete picture of the self that is publicly offered, like a person huddled behind a cardboard cutout likeness of himself, fearful of discovery. Obviously, such a person is not seeking any approval from the God who can see behind any façade that may be constructed. Rather, such a person is motivated by the possibility of approval from other people, who often can be deceived.

The doubter who does those things associated with belief may be similarly motivated in some instances. To be sure, the temptation is less for us in our day than it was in Jesus' day because such a show of piety is less likely to be rewarded with sufficient praise to motivate us. Yet it is important to admit that the temptation may still exist, because there are certain circumstances and circles in which we might receive praise for merely acting as if we believe or as if we have put our faith in God. We know, at the very least, that we do much for appearances in other aspects of our lives. Indeed, our age, as Kierkegaard said of his, is so concerned with appearances that we will "sell our trousers to buy a wig." We will sometimes pay exclusive attention to the side of our lives that is visible to others. Because it is easy. Because it works. Because we can often fool one another.

It must be granted, then, that a person in our age may still do those things normally associated with belief while holding grave doubts because he or she is motivated by some potential rewards that might be received from others. That reward might be in the form of praise. But the possible reward for public expressions of belief, such as weekly attendance at worship, are usually of a different order. I know of one young businesswoman who was told during her first month of work with a major corporation that it would be helpful for her to join a church because attendance at worship provides unique opportunities to establish helpful business contacts. Such a prospect affords considerable motivation. More likely, however, the promise of reward will be subtle, such as the assurance that if one attends worship, one will have conformed to the expectations within a particular family or community. Such motivations are more rare in our day than is commonly supposed, but they still exist. Depending on the circumstances, then, a person who makes a public show of belief while holding doubts may be properly described as a hypocrite, but only if that person is motivated by the promise of personal gain from others.

The Desire for Belief

Nevertheless, it is important to note that there are other motivations entirely that can be at work in the person who doubts and yet participates in common expressions of belief. It has nothing to do with the reactions of others. No willful deception is at work. Rather, the motivation is the yearning for belief, a hope for a living faith in God. A person may attend worship because he or she has an unspoken yet urgent question that theologian Karl Barth identified as the question that brings people to worship, "Is it true?" It is a question that person may have been able to answer in the affirmative, on occasion at least, but that must be asked again and again because the answer can never be accepted as definitive. A person may come with a mixture of belief and doubt, yet desire that whatever belief he or she brings might be addressed and nurtured.

Again, if we are properly to discern if hypocrisy is at work, we must look to motives. Consider expressions of charity. On the one hand, it is possible that if you are struck on the right cheek, you will turn your other cheek in the sole hope that you will be praised for restraint and moral superiority. It is also conceivable that if someone steals your coat, you will offer the thief your shirt as well because of a desire to be seen by others as generous. If one is motivated by the promise of praise from others, even in acts of charity, one might be properly described as a hypocrite.

On the other hand, another motivation entirely may be at work that has nothing to do with the praise of others. You might turn the other cheek or give a thief the shirt off your back in order to act charitably. Carefully note that this does not necessarily mean that you *feel* charitable. Jesus did not say that when a person hits you on the cheek that you should feel charitable toward the person. Rather, he said that when a person hits you on the cheek you should forget about your feelings for a moment and act charitably by turning to that person your other cheek. Likewise, Jesus could have said that when a person steals your coat you should feel all sorts of good things about the thief. But no, Jesus said that if a person steals your coat, offer that person your shirt as well. You may not feel like doing, it, you may not have any of the charitable feelings that are normally associated with such an act, but do it anyway.

Jesus does not ask us to feel charitable before acting charitably because feelings are notoriously slow. If someone has just struck you in the face, the time to act cannot be postponed. Sometimes the expression of charity is all that we can muster. Also, feelings, unlike actions, cannot be governed by simple will. If Jesus were asking us to feel charitable toward a person before acting charitably, he would be asking something that is not within our control, not after his teachings, not after his example, not after his commands. We simply cannot feel on command. Jesus was wise enough not to ask that of us. Instead, he asks us to act, and that is within our control. Turn your cheek. Give your shirt. Pray for your enemies. Worship God. Do not wait until you feel like doing it. Just do it. At the very least, it is by acting charitably that we give charitable feelings a chance to grow. But further, and this is the most important point, it is by acting charitably that feelings of charity are best nurtured. It is by expressing charity that we can come to feel charitable.

Similarly, we may worship before feeling particularly worshipful, pray before we feel in the least prayerful, and express belief without yet fully believing. Such expressions may be motivated by the desire to prepare for the advent of worshipfulness, prayerfulness, and firmer belief. C. S. Lewis drew this comparison: When we carry out "religious duties," we are like people digging channels in a waterless land in order that, when the water finally comes, it might find the channels ready. Perhaps we can go a step further: When we practice what Lewis calls "religious duties," it is not as something to do in the interim between our expressions of belief and the advent of belief. Rather, it can be through such expressions that we come to experience those things expressed. In other words, if we are digging channels, it is not just so they might be ready when at last the water comes; by digging such channels we create a landscape that is more likely to find the presence of water. It is by worship that we can come to know the experience of worshipfulness. It is through the practice of prayer that we can come to affirm the efficacy of prayer. It is in joining public affirmations of belief that we can come to recognize the truth in them. In some instances, "saying is believing." In all these things we can act as if we believe in order to believe, or believe more fully.

Acting in Faith

Actors have long understood this dynamic interaction between outward behavior and inner responses. Let us assume that an actress is called upon to portray a person who is consumed with anger. One way for the actress accurately to portray such a character would be for her to get in touch with feelings of anger within herself, to remember times when she has been angry, to feel again what she once felt. If this inner work is done properly, the character will exhibit anger most convincingly. There will be great verisimilitude in the performance.

Another way to play a part pays no attention to inner reactions but concentrates on outward behavior. In this instance, the actress simply recreates those things she would normally do to express anger. The result will also be a convincing performance, but something else will result. By acting out the behavior commonly associated with anger, she will feel anger.

Although we may not be professional actors, we can experience some of this same dynamic. First, try sitting in a relaxed, calm manner. Release all the tension from your muscles. Then stand up and do some of those things that you would do to express anger. Clench your fists. Take deep breaths. Squint your eyes. Pace back and forth. Raise your voice. Before you know it, you will be angry! You may not know what you are angry about, but you will be angry nonetheless. The feeling is unmistakable. It is there because you have expressed it.

It is important to add that the anger is not created out of thin air. It must exist somewhere in the experience of the individual for it to be expressed accurately or for it to be felt upon being expressed. So too, expressions of belief cannot produce belief out of nothing. Rather, such expressions can only help us discover the measure of belief that is within us. We can express full belief in order to nurture the growth of any tender bud of belief we may have.

It is this understanding that helps us make sense out of Frederick Buechner's unlikely advice to those who would approach the Lord's Supper:

> It is make-believe. You make believe that the one who breaks the bread and blesses the wine is not the plump parson who smells of Williams's Aqua Velva but Jesus of Nazareth. You make believe that the tasteless wafer and cheap port are his flesh and blood. You make believe that by swallowing them you are swallowing his life into your life and that there is nothing in earth or heaven more important for you to do than this. It is a game you play because He said to play it. "Do this in remembrance of Me." Do *this*. Play that it makes a difference. Play that it makes sense. If it seems a childish thing to do, do it in remembrance that you are a child.[1]

Is Buechner here advising us to make believe that the Lord's Supper makes a difference as part of some empty charade? Not at all. We may first approach the Lord's Supper because we are told to do so, or because we are willing to give this game a try, but we may soon find something else bringing us to the table. These outer expressions allow for a transformation of our inner experience. In this, as in so much in the life of faith, we may start with a game of make-believe only so that, in time, we might discover that we do indeed believe.

That this was Buechner's intent is made clear when he follows his advice with a recounting of Max Beerbohm's tale of the "Happy Hypocrite." In Beerbohm's story a wicked man loved a virtuous girl. The man knew that he could not hope to woo her if he approached her undisguised, so he donned the mask of a saint. Sure enough, the girl fell in love with the man, or perhaps we should say she fell in love with the saintly mask. Years later, when a spurned lover of the man discovered the deception, she challenged the hypocrite to shed his mask in front of his beloved and show his face for the ugly, repulsive thing it was. When, after considerable protest, he dropped his mask, he discovered what he could not have anticipated: Under the mask of the saint his face had become transformed. It was the face of a saint.

Beerbohm correctly labeled the character in his story a "hypocrite," for clearly it was the man's intention to deceive. Yet even when such a man acted the part of saint, a transformation took place. Beerbohm's story is just a fairy tale. Nevertheless, something similar can take place within those who assume the costume of belief, not as a deceitful disguise, but in order to be inwardly transformed to its likeness. Such a costume may not fit very snugly at first. It may balloon in just the places where it should fit smartly. It may be so bulky that it makes the wearer feel awkward. But as every child who has been fitted for shoes has been told, it is important to have "room to grow." What seems to cause you to trip all over yourself today allows the possibility for growth.

Paul urged the members of the church in Rome to "put on" Christ." We have come to associate the expression "put on" with a willful deception, such as when we might say of some ruse, "It was all just a put-on." But, of course, that is not what Paul had in mind. He was asking his listeners to assume some of the qualities of Christ, to wear them as they would a new and perhaps ill-fitting set of clothes, in order that some day they might fit and be fitting expressions of who they had become.

On the one hand, a hypocrite who dons the costume of belief in the hope of personal gain, praying in order to be seen praying, worshiping in order to garner the approval of others, will be fearful of discovery. On the other hand, a person who prays or worships while still holding doubts about these very activities, and yet is motivated by the desire to grow in belief and find a trusting faith in God, will have no such fears. Because it is not the approval of others that is sought, and there is no attempt to deceive, such a person can be very open with his or her doubt. There is no need to pretend that the costume is a perfect fit or that it is worn under all circumstances.

Exploring Doubt

It is important for those who doubt and yet yearn to believe to find appropriate and helpful settings in which to explore their doubt and give it full expression. There are times when the shadow of our doubt needs to see the light of day. Often those who hold serious religious doubts are reluctant to express them, especially within the context of the church. Sometimes they feel alone in their doubts and fear that if their expressions of doubt do not find an echo in the hearts of others, they will find themselves further isolated. Other times people are afraid that expressing their most serious doubts is to unleash them with a new kind of power. Usually, however, quite the opposite is true. If people share their doubts within an honest and trusting environment, they will find that doubt is virtually universal among mere human beings, and they will gain both insight and strength from the discovery. If people openly express their doubts, they can find those doubts becoming less threatening in the process because doubts, like mushrooms, grow best in the dark. Also, an honest expression of doubt can reassure us that we are not posing as something we are not, that we are not hypocrites.

There are other times, however, when it is helpful to cease any examinations of our doubt, at least momentarily. There is, indeed, a time for every purpose under heaven: a time to examine our doubts and a time to give our doubts a rest. For instance, although various parts of a worship service may directly address or acknowledge our doubts, worship is primarily an opportunity to express belief in God and to seek a full and living faith. Worship is not a time for the Christian story to be reduced to the least common denominator of belief, that is, reduced to those aspects of the story that are believed by every person present. A worship service reduced in this way would be very brief indeed! Also, such a worship service, like a costume that fits all too snugly, would not leave room for growth in belief or encourage such growth.

Instead, worship is a time to give full expression to the historic beliefs of the church, whether or not the people present are fully convinced of their truth. It is a time to say to the biblical witness and the historic testimony of the church what Goethe, in *Conversations with Eckermann*, once said to a friend, "Tell me of your faith; I have doubt enough of my own." It is a time to assume an attitude of prayer, even if we have doubts about the efficacy of prayer. It is a time to praise the acts of God, even if we hold more doubt than belief about the very acts of which we sing or speak.

Obviously, it is not possible, or even desirable, to leave our doubts at the door of the church. Many, however, go much further: They give their doubts center stage during worship. Although they come with a mixture of doubt and belief, as almost all worshipers do, they give their doubt virtually undivided attention. They do not assume an attitude of receptivity. They do not don the costume of belief long enough to grow into it.

Some people are unwilling to leave their critical faculties unused for even a moment. They are always on guard against credulity. They arm themselves with skepticism and clutch it with white-knuckled determination. One reason for their vigilance is the fear that, if they were to abandon their critical faculties, they could come to believe almost anything. They want certainty before entrusting themselves to the Christian God. They want no part of anything that even sounds as if it might approach brainwashing. They have heard stories about those who have come to believe the most twisted and silly things because they dropped their skepticism and put themselves in the hands of a cult leader. Yet this kind of brainwashing is very different from what is being suggested here. For those who seek to believe, or believe more fully, in the Christian God, doubt is not forbidden expression, as it is in most cults. The critical faculties are not utterly abandoned. There is no coercion, not even coercion from the self, because ultimately one cannot make oneself believe.

Under such circumstances we cannot be led to believe just anything. What we can do is take on the Christian religion as a kind of working hypothesis, something that is to be assumed for a time to allow for further exploration. It is an attitude of receptivity that invites further discovery and growth. The assumption of the Christian hypothesis can help us explore what we can, in fact, believe. This attitude of receptivity will help us discover whatever belief might reside, dormant or hidden, within us and allow that belief to grow.

To some the suggestion that they assume an expression of belief in order to give that belief an opportunity to grow can sound like the advice to Alice by the White Queen in *Through the Looking Glass*:

> The Queen remarked: "Now I'll give *you* something to believe. I'm just one hundred and one, five months and a day."
>
> "I can't believe *that!*" said Alice.
>
> "Can't you?" the Queen said in a pitying tone. "Try again: draw a long breath, and shut your eyes."

Alice laughed. "There's no use trying," she said: "I simply can't believe impossible things."

"I daresay you haven't had much practice," said the Queen. "When I was your age, I always believed as many as six impossible things before breakfast."[2]

There are those for whom the Christian story is as impossible to believe as it was impossible for Alice to believe the Queen's claim that she was "one hundred and one, five months and a day." The story of a God who acted in history and is still alive and at work in the world, of a God who cares and cares about them, of a God who shared our lives in the person of a baby born in a stable in a small corner of a big world is, for some, simply impossible to believe. For such people, no amount of what the Queen called "practice" will make them believe. It is impossible to believe things that seem forever and always impossible.

But for those whom Pascal described as "seeing too much to deny and too little to be sure," something else is possible. They have a mixture of doubt and belief; the mixture is variously proportioned depending on the time and circumstance. To be sure, they cannot make themselves believe. What they can do is discover and awaken whatever measure of belief they may already have. They can, in the words of 2 Timothy 6:1, "stir up the gift of God" that is within them.

Indeed, this is achieved through something like practice, through what has been called "practicing the presence of God." Such practice does not include the taking of deep breaths and the closing of one's eyes. Rather, it is living in faith to give belief a chance. This means entrusting oneself to God's care through faith, the care of the same God about whom one maintains considerable doubt. The practice of Christian faith includes praying with an open and receptive heart. It means approaching the communion table in the desire that one might discover, and then feast on, the presence of God. It includes giving resounding voice to the praise of God that may only whisper within us. It is acting as if the people around us are God's children even though we are used to seeing them as only the people around us.

In these and similar ways, we will indeed become practicing Christians. Practicing the Christian faith is like other forms of practice in that there is the need for repetition and much patience. Often our attempts will be faltering. There may be days when it feels almost easy followed by other days in which it feels surely futile. A sense of humor about our own efforts is almost essential.

The willingness to practice belief while waiting to believe is, in itself, something like an expression of faith. It is a step taken in trust. Such practice is undertaken in the desire to discover if there is truth in what we affirm, to find out if what we do as if it is true might become, in time, what we do because it is true.

Questions for Reflection

+ Should our actions and beliefs always be consistent?

+ Have you ever felt like a hypocrite when engaging in religious practice? According to the definitions in this chapter, do you think you actually were being a hypocrite?

+ What, specifically, would it look like for you to "put on Christ" in your life?

+ Have you ever acted your way into a new way of thinking?

CHAPTER FIVE

Actively Awaiting Belief

As THIS CHAPTER BEGINS, it must raise yet another point that may be discouraging, at least initially: We can prepare ourselves to receive the gift of belief by "practicing" the Christian faith, but practice is not enough in itself to ensure that we will one day believe. This chapter will consider some of the specific steps we can take to prepare ourselves to receive the gift of belief. Those steps can be summarized in one word: "wait." We can wait. We can wait to receive the gift of belief. We can only wait.

Is there any more discouraging word in our vocabulary than the word "wait"? No one likes to wait. Waiting can make us impatient and irritable. We will go to almost any extreme to escape waiting. Many of us would rather drive fifteen minutes out of our way to avoid waiting five minutes in traffic. We want to be up and doing. It is the passivity we associate with waiting that perhaps bothers us the most, as Henri Nouwen points out:

> Most of us think of waiting as something very passive, a hopeless state determined by events totally out of our hands. The bus is late? You cannot do anything about it, so you have to sit there and just wait. It is not difficult to understand the irritation people feel when somebody says, "Just wait." Words like that seem to push us into passivity.[1]

As a boy, if I were walking home from school and saw a friend walking ahead, I would shout out his name and call "Wait!" The friend would stop. But when I got closer I would say, "Don't just stand there, wait for me!" It was a popular joke among boys of my day because, to us, waiting and just standing there were really the same thing. You could do something or you could just stand there and wait.

Active versus Passive Waiting

What we did not understand as boys is that there are different kinds of waiting. Some waiting *is* passive. But there is also active waiting. A girl who stands on a street corner waiting for the bus to arrive will experience one kind of waiting, a passive waiting. That same girl on the same corner hearing the sound of a parade that is just out of sight will also wait, but it will be a different kind of waiting, full of expectation, a waiting on tip-toe, an active waiting.

A fisherman experiences the difference between passive waiting and active waiting. A fisherman finds it burdensome to wait for spring to arrive and fishing season to begin, but once he is fishing, he does not find it a burden to wait for the trout to rise to his fly, and in many ways the waiting itself is delicious. The difference is that one kind of waiting is passive and the other is active. In the dead of winter, the fisherman can do nothing but passively wait for time to pass. But at the pool of his favorite trout stream his waiting is filled with accomplishing all the many things he must do, all injected with an active sense of anticipation.

We can choose to wait passively for the gift of belief. We can live our lives as if the world were a waiting room, not merely flipping through magazines, to be sure, but generally filling the time with whatever is at hand, occupying ourselves with the tasks of the day. We may assume that an all-knowing God knows where to find us if God ever wants us. Such passive waiting does not require much in the way of our attention or

[handwritten marginal note: Overstated: The fisherman could be making lures.]

energy. It leaves us completely free to concentrate on the concerns of the moment.

Or we can activate our waiting for the gift of belief. We can wait as the psalmist waits: "I wait for the Lord, my soul waits, and in his word I hope; my soul waits for the Lord more than those who watch for the morning" (Psalm 130:5-6). It is a waiting that is filled with eager expectation. It is through this kind of active waiting, through what the psalmist called "waiting for the Lord," that we can be prepared to receive the gift of belief.

Those who actively wait for belief will put themselves in a place where God is apt to draw near. To be sure, God can confront us at the check-out line in the supermarket or on the eighth hole of the golf course. It is also true that God can seem distant and elusive within a church. Nevertheless, it is when we take on Christian practices as a kind of working hypothesis that we are more likely to discover the truth in them. Those who wait passively for belief need not be concerned with prayer, worship, mission, scriptural study, or any of the other ways in which one acts out the Christian life. But those who wait actively for belief will be involved in all of those things. It is a waiting that is spent in service, more like a waiter who "waits" on an important visitor than it is like a person nodding off in a waiting room. There is much to be done in such waiting, and there is no time to sit down and count the tips.

The Company of Believers

The person who actively waits for belief will also seek out the company of those who believe in God and trust in God through faith. People who believe in God cannot teach us to believe. People who exhibit a living relationship with God through their faith cannot transfer their attitude to us in any sure or immediate way. But those who put their faith in God—that is, those who entrust God with their lives; those who seek to know, serve, and honor God—can live lives of such allure and attractiveness that we are sufficiently encouraged to emulate them. We may not yet be able to think or feel as they do, but in acting as they do, we leave ourselves open to the stirrings of belief that may be within us.

Someone once told me about taking a winter hike in the woods. As he tells the story, he found himself standing at the edge of a frozen river, needing to cross it but afraid that the ice was not thick enough to support him. Drawing on a dim recollection of something he had learned in high school physics, he decided to distribute his weight on a larger area of ice by lying on his stomach and slithering across. As he proceeded off the bank a few feet, ever so slowly and in great fear, he heard something that he came to recognize as the sound of sleigh bells ringing and people singing. Then he saw a huge sled loaded with wood, a man and his whole family singing Christmas carols, coming across the ice. They waved at the man who was lying prostrate on the ice. Feeling quite foolish, he pretended for a moment to be looking through the ice before he stood up, brushed the snow off his clothes, and proceeded across the river with new confidence.

People of faith can do something similar for us. It is only by entrusting ourselves to God's care through faith that we can know that God is worthy of our trust. Of course, we may do everything that we observe the person of faith doing and still not find that our actions are filled with the conviction of the person who believes in God. Nevertheless, through their example people of faith can give us the courage to travel the same road and discover for ourselves that the way is sure. We can observe and follow examples of faith in the hope and expectation that, in time, we will come to believe in the God to whom we are entrusting ourselves.

People of faith do more than simply attract us to the life of faith in some general way. After all, the ways of faith are manifold, and the commitment of faith is lived out in the full range of ways one can order one's life: in the way one views the world, makes decisions, responds to life's joys and hardships, even in the way one spends each day. So examples of faith are not discovered, tapped for inspiration, and then discarded. Because the ways of faith are so subtle and multifarious, there is always more to learn from such examples.

Even as we seek the company of those who believe and attempt to follow their example, it is important to be open with our doubts. That, too, is a part of active waiting. Unexpressed doubts are particularly potent. Doubts prosper in the hidden, dark places where they can be left undisturbed. This fact has been touched on already. Little more remains to be said here, except perhaps to give an example from my own experience. One evening, during my second year of divinity school, I was reading the Bible in preparation for a sermon I was to deliver the next Sunday. The passage I was reading was a particularly unlikely story—which one, I cannot now remember—and on this occasion it seemed like just one of the most ridiculous things I had ever read. And I felt quite ridiculous even reading it. Gone was the way the Bible had stirred me in the past. Gone, too, was the certainty that there was no other way for me to live my life than to serve God and spread the gospel. What was left was this curious book with the solemn black binding. Disillusioned, I tossed it across my desk. It was at that moment, before I had turned to do anything else, that a close friend and classmate came to the door. He could see I was disturbed and asked what was happening. I was reluctant to tell him because he had always been for me an example of faith I greatly admired and from whom I had learned much. But the power of my experience of doubt overwhelmed any hesitation

I might have had, so I told him. I remember being afraid that I might shock him. I think I half expected him to ask, "Can I help you pack your books, because you obviously don't belong here in divinity school anymore?" But instead, he said, "I know. Something like that happened to me just last week."

My friend's response did not magnify my sense of uncertainty. Quite the opposite: That experience, and countless others, showed me that there are times when expressing our doubts to one another can be more helpful than sharing our beliefs. If, in response to my doubts, my friend had offered a testimony to his own beliefs, or told me why my doubts were unfounded, or had otherwise given me a pep talk, propped me up, and sent me on my way, I would not have been helped nearly as much. I was helped by expressing my doubts and having them heard by an accepting friend. I was helped further by hearing that this person of strong beliefs also experienced similar doubts and that he had not packed his bags the first time those doubts appeared. It is ironic, perhaps, but true nonetheless, that there are times when expressing our doubts can be the best way to nurture our belief.

Opening Up to God

We can go a step further. Those who actively wait for belief will not only share their doubts with one another but will also share their doubts with God. This may sound like odd advice. If we have doubts, the last one we are likely to tell is God. It seems an absurdity for us to tell God that we are not sure God exists or that we are uncertain that God has power. The part of us that does not believe in God has no God to turn to, while the part of us that does believe in God also hesitates to share doubt, as if we are protecting God from our doubt. We think God would be shocked by our doubt.

Once again we should remember the father who turned to Jesus for help with the words, "I believe; help my unbelief" (Mark 9:24). The man doubted the very one he was looking to for help. Jesus was not shocked. He responded by granting the man's request, even though the request was qualified with doubt. Likewise, God is not shocked if we doubt that God has power or question whether God even exists. Surely, God has seen too much to be shocked anymore. A God who is big enough to prompt our doubts is big enough to handle those doubts.

People call on God when they are in greatest need, and where is our need greater than in our struggle to believe in God? Many times we find it difficult to pray because our doubts get in the way. We may hardly begin to pray before our words trail off, our minds racing with doubt. But those who entrust God with their doubts might use their doubts as an occasion for prayer. Such a prayer might begin in this way: "Dear God . . . I don't know what I mean when I address you in that way. I'm not even sure I believe you exist. It's so hard to believe with all of the things that are going on in my life right now. I want to believe in you, God, but you are not making it very easy. . . ." In this way, rather than keeping us from prayer, our doubts can be the subject of prayer. Rather than ending prayer, doubts can be the beginning point of prayer. God is interested not in being presented with our best selves but with our true selves, including our doubts. When we offer God our doubts in prayer, it is in the hope that, with the alchemy of God's care, our doubts will be transformed into fuller belief.

Those who pray in this way may find their belief bolstered, but they cannot expect to overcome their doubt completely. This should not surprise us. The experience of belief is almost never found unalloyed. Belief and doubt are almost always found together and in inextricable ways. Another part of active

waiting is to recognize this. We need to know what we are waiting for: If we wait for all doubt to be obliterated, we are in for a
long wait. Only very rarely is a human lifetime long enough to
have such an unqualified experience of belief. Instead, we can
actively wait for the kind of belief that may still be qualified by
doubt but that is not utterly paralyzed by doubt. We can understand the difference through a paraphrase of Robert Browning, who described one person's conversion as exchanging a
life of doubt diversified by belief, for one of belief diversified
by doubt. This is no small distinction. It not only implies what
understanding, doubt or belief, will dominate our thinking.
It also implies how we will act, whether we will seek ways to
increase our doubt or our belief, whether we will try on Christian practices or leave them on the shelf, whether we privately
despair because our doubts are so strong or pray to God that
our belief might be strengthened.

Belief Diversified by Doubt

If we live a life that can be described as one of belief diversified by doubt, we may have times when we are momentarily
convinced that doubt is in retreat, if not yet defeated alto-
gether. Our belief may be quickened inexplicably by a sense
of wonder or awe. We may be spontaneously inspired to reverence by something we observe or experience or for reasons
that remain mysterious even to us. At such times our belief
can seem robust, indefatigable, even easy. These are valuable
times, as important as time spent in a desert oasis, when we
can refresh ourselves and prepare for the rest of the journey.
Such times are to be received as graciously as they are given.

Nevertheless, there is a danger in experiencing such times
as well, for our time in a spiritual oasis can all too easily con-
vince us that we can expect to spend all of our time in such

welcome and hospitable surroundings. If we think the oasis is the final destination, it can be more than a little discouraging to learn that we must again plod through the desert. Once such epiphanies of belief pass, as they inevitably will, we can become preoccupied with concern for how to recreate such experiences and despair when that seems impossible. Like the character in a Dylan Thomas play who was kissed once behind the pigsty when she wasn't looking and was never kissed again, though she was looking all the time, the person who has been overcome by an experience of belief of great power is often later discouraged when the experience is not repeated, or at least not with any consistency or predictability. And such times can persuade us of the mistaken notion that belief will be found only in such unequivocal experiences that are free from doubt.

In short, moments when belief asserts itself almost to the point of certainty can prevent us from recognizing the truth that governs most of our experience: Doubt and belief are almost always inextricably intertwined. We cannot expect belief to be found without the company of doubt, and if we do have moments when belief is found in blissful solitude, we cannot expect such times to last. Instead, we need to expect that doubt and belief will be found together, and that there will be times when we are more acutely aware of our doubt than our belief. This is true even in a life that could be described as one of belief diversified by doubt. After all, minority parties are sometimes the most vocal in any passionate debate.

Whatever the current mixture of doubt and belief in a person's life, those who actively await fuller belief will, in the words of Harry Emerson Fosdick, "believe in as much God as [they] can." Such people will freely recognize their doubts but choose instead to focus on their beliefs. David Roberts quotes one man who told him, "I spent twenty years trying to come to terms with my doubts. Then one day it dawned on me that I had better come to terms with my faith. Now I have passed from the agony of questions I cannot answer into the agony of answers I cannot escape. And it's a great relief."[2] Or as one old wag put it to me, "Houses have dark basements and attics—but we don't have to live in them."

Beyond focusing on their beliefs, such people will act on whatever beliefs they have. Kierkegaard remarked that he thought it strange that people complained that there was much in the Bible they could not accept when there was enough that they could accept to keep them busy for a lifetime. Indeed, it is true that if we cannot accept some of the larger claims of the gospel, for most of us there are portions that we can accept without too much difficulty. But even if we recognize that we have enough belief to act on, still we may not jump at the opportunity to do so. This is not surprising: Great humility is required of the beginner. It is difficult to take a stand in the corner of our belief when we feel surrounded by doubt. Besides, it is always easier to put off commitment than it is to act.

Mark Twain may have been making a similar point when he confessed that the portions of the Bible that disturbed him the most were not the parts he did not understand but the ones he *did* understand. And why did those portions disturb him? Certainly, in part, because he had to act on them. He could not postpone acting on them by seeking refuge in the facile claim that he was confused or uncertain.

Of course, focusing on those things we can believe and acting on them is not an end in itself. Rather, we start from whatever corner of belief we have so that, in time, as we gain in experience and confidence, we might work from that corner to wider circles of belief.

All the while it is important for those who actively await belief to be patient with those things they cannot yet understand or accept. It is difficult to leave questions unanswered, especially when they concern us so profoundly. It takes great humility to recognize the limits of our understanding, to doubt our own firmly held beliefs with the same thoroughness with which we sometimes doubt the beliefs of others. It takes considerable courage to admit, with Thomas Edison, "We do not know one millionth of one percent about anything."

We all have files in our minds labeled "Accepted" and "Rejected." As we hear or think about something, we usually feel obliged to relegate this new item to one or the other file. We may ask ourselves, "Can I believe this passage of scripture records something that actually happened?" And again we feel obliged to put our conclusion in one file or the other. Or, again, we may ask, "Can I believe this particular tenet of the Christian faith?" We may hesitate for a moment, but after all, we must do something with such scraps. They cannot just lie around cluttering our lives and confusing us, so we choose one file or the other and put it in.

Those who actively wait for belief will still have files in their minds labeled "Rejected" and "Accepted." But they will also have a large and active file labeled "Awaiting Further Light." Obviously, such a file will not be found in the mind of a fanatic (the person who could be described as the one who believes what God would believe if God had all the facts). Those who make liberal use of the file labeled "Awaiting Further Light" exhibit a humility that is not found in the fanatic believer or disbeliever. The presence of such a file demonstrates a posture of openness to new truth and unfolding experience. Such a file will be filled with all those things that do not yet clearly belong in either the "Accepted" file or the "Rejected" file. For those who actively wait to believe in the Christian God, such a file may also include many items of traditional Christian beliefs about God that we would be inclined to put in the "Rejected" file were it not for the voices of historic Christian witnesses that seem to be whispering, "Not so fast. You may not fully believe this now, but please trust us enough to put it somewhere you will be sure to consider it again."

In this process of sorting out what we can believe and what we cannot, it is important not to try to force ourselves to believe. As Emily Dickinson put it, "Believing what we don't believe does not exhilarate" (Poem 1741). Clearly this is poetic understatement. Trying to make ourselves believe not only fails to exhilarate, it can have many deleterious effects. The White Queen told Alice that all she had to do to believe was to hold her breath and shut her eyes. If we tried to follow this advice, certainly we would turn blue before our belief increased. Trying to force ourselves to believe can be dangerous to our health. It is futile. Attempting it will only lead to disappointment, or worse. When our best efforts to force belief fail, we may become convinced that all belief is an illusion and give up in despair. Even active waiting requires a healthy dose of patience.

Rainer Maria Rilke once gave this famous advice to a young poet: "I want to beg you to be patient toward all that is unsolved in your heart and try to love the questions themselves."[3] For those who urgently seek answers to their religious doubts, questions seldom appear lovable. Questions seem to stand between us and that which we seek. To our frequent frustration, the questions seem unwilling to step aside and we are unable to push them away.

Nevertheless, those who actively wait to believe in God can still find some satisfactions in the wait itself. The active wait for fuller belief may not be enough to sustain us forever, but it may be enough for now. Again, we might think of the fisherman waiting for the rise of a trout or of the person on tiptoe waiting for the parade to pass for whom active waiting is full and absorbing.

It is also important to remember that the ultimate goal of our waiting is not to be finally convinced of some intellectual proposition about the existence or nature of God. Rather, beyond these things, that which we seek, that for which our hearts are restless, is a living relationship with God. Beyond answers, we seek a presence, the fuller presence of God in our lives. We may have more patience with our waiting if we recognize that it is very much like waiting for a relationship to grow and become more fully established, as Mary McDermott Shideler observed:

> Even in strictly human relationships, it is a good rule to take it easy, not to force things, not to hurry, but to enjoy the slow ripening of friendship or love. All the more, our relation (with God) develops at its own pace, seasons of laughter alternating with seasons of intensity and of indifference. They are all part of the process and of the pattern, all to be welcomed as aspects of the breakthrough of the barriers between us and God.[4]

All these are ways in which we can actively await belief. They are not techniques that, if mastered, ensure that we will find the object of our waiting. As active as our waiting for belief may be, it is still waiting. When we are waiting for belief we are waiting for something that can be given to us only by God. But, unlike what I assumed when I was a boy, there is a big difference between waiting and just standing around. If our waiting is active, we can become as sensitive to the tiptoeing presence of God as we are sensitive to our longing for that presence. We may even discover that throughout our search for God it was really God who was searching for us all along.

Questions for Reflection

◆ What are some additional examples of the difference between passive waiting and active waiting?

◆ In what ways has the faith of other people had an impact on your own faith?

◆ Using Robert Browning's terminology, do you currently live a life of faith diversified by doubt, or a life of doubt diversified by faith?

◆ If we all have files in our minds labeled "Accepted," "Rejected," and "Awaiting Further Light," what is an example of something in your own life that you have moved from one file to another?

CHAPTER SIX

Doubt and Decision

Is THERE ANYONE MORE NONCOMMITTAL than a young teenager at his or her first dance? We have all seen them; most likely, at one time we were there ourselves. They stand around the edge of the dance hall as far from the opposite sex as possible. They are all hands and can find no place to put them. Their faces struggle to be casual. The look says, "Don't think I came here on purpose. Somehow I just ended up in this place."

If we happened to look in on this scene, we might well wonder: "What are they waiting for, anyway? Waiting for the right song? Waiting for the right girl or boy to look in their direction? Waiting to become a few years older?"

Jesus said that the people of his generation, like modern teenagers, did not know what they wanted. First they were suspicious of John the Baptist because of his severe, otherworldly asceticism. Then they were suspicious of Jesus because of his seemingly carefree worldliness. So they simple refused to dance to the tune of either John or Jesus (Luke 7:31–34).

They were like people of a later day who attend a dance but sit in chairs around the edge of the hall for the entire evening. They listen attentively through waltz, fox trot, tango, jitterbug, without so much as tapping a toe. Finally, the piano player decides he has had enough. He stands up, puts his hands on his hips, and asks with volume, "Hey, what do you folks want anyway?"

The seated dancers may reply, "We're waiting for our song," but when they are asked what that song is, they can only giggle and say, "We'll know it when we hear it." The frustrated piano player soon suspects they have come to sit all along, that sitting around the edge of the dance floor is their idea of a good time.

An Invitation to Dance

Jesus uses the image of dance as an expression of commitment. It is an unlikely image but a profound once. You do not have to be in middle school to know that a dance floor can be a frightening place, even under the best of circumstances. There is that moment of hesitation: "Who will be the first to go out there and dance? I sure don't want to be the only one. What if all of these people are really classy dancers? I don't want to look foolish. What if I step on someone's toes? This song has a strange beat; maybe the next one will be easier to dance to."

But in Jesus' image this is not just any dance, and it is not the usual music. The one playing the music is Jesus himself, and he asks nothing less than we dance to it. He is asking that we stop thinking of ourselves as spectators. He is asking that we dance, that we let him call the tune for our lives. In short, he is presenting us with an invitation that requires a decision. Obviously, this can make us uncomfortable. We would prefer to stay in our seats, and we can offer countless reasons for our reluctance to do otherwise. We may protest that our doubts prevent us from responding. Our doubts are strong and sticky and seem to hold us in our seats. After all, we are the ones who find it difficult to comply with the exhortation of the old hymn "Stand Up for Jesus." Surely it is too much to expect us to dance for him! We are not ready. Let us sit through another song or two. If we simply "Stand Up for Jesus" and it gets to be a bit much, we can always pretend that we stood up to stretch our legs. But to dance! That is different, and much more difficult. When we dance we are really committing ourselves. There is no turning back. We are dancing all right, and there is no use in trying to pass it off as something else.

When Jesus asks for our commitment by using the image of dance, he is not asking that we resolve all doubt before taking such a step. He is not asking that we feel confident. He is not asking that we think ourselves qualified. He is not even asking that we like the music. In fact, Jesus is not addressing himself to how we think or feel, because none of that is immediately within our control. Instead, he is asking us to act, to take a step in faith, a step onto the dance floor. He is asking us to join the dance, to do our best to move in step with his music, to kick up our heels in spite of our hesitations or doubts.

By focusing on how we act rather than how we think or feel, Jesus eliminates some of our favorite excuses for avoiding commitment. Sometimes when we stay in our seats we claim that it is because we are simply waiting for the right tune, but the truth is that we simply do not want to dance. We avoid decision by claiming that our doubts prevent us from making a commitment. Then Jesus calls our bluff by telling us to bring our doubts onto the dance floor.

Now, to be sure, we know from our own experience that doubts can be painful. We can seek to rid ourselves of them. But if we are honest with ourselves, we will have to admit that there are other times when we seek refuge in our doubts. If we do not want to dance, that is, if we want to avoid commitment, our doubts can provide a convenient excuse for staying in our seats. In this way our doubts can serve us well. By claiming that we are a slave to our doubts, we can avoid the call to be servants of Christ.

Self-serving Doubts

When we conclude that our doubts prevent us from making a commitment to God, we must eventually face this difficult question: Is it possible that those doubts are self-serving, that we use them in an attempt to escape the necessity of commitment? Doubts may seem to cling to us, but there are times when we can cling to our doubts. Although doubt may be difficult, we can sometimes use it as a pretext for avoiding the even more difficult step of commitment. We may press our doubts into service in an attempt to fight off the time of decision. We want to defend our comfortable way of life at almost all costs, a way of life defined in the cynic's creed: "Consider all, commit to little, keep moving."

It is common to hear the objection that in religious matters, the language of decision is too confining to reflect the ambiguity of our experience. Such language is so very black-and-white when our experience of God is most often in a shade of gray. Many students prefer "true or false" questions on a test because even if they have absolutely no idea which is the correct answer they still have an even chance of guessing it correctly. But in religious matters a true/false, either/or decision is discomforting. The decision is too absolute, too starkly presented, the choices too few. When faced with the need for decision we are tempted to ask, "Don't you have any essay questions?" We want to be able to qualify our answers. We want to be able to say, "Yes, but on the other hand. . . ."

So those who are uncomfortable with the language of decision often substitute words that emphasize evolutionary growth in their understanding of God and their relationship with God. They employ images such as "pilgrimage" or "spiritual journey." Instead of arriving at a decision, they are perpetually en route. They are not ready to decide, but they are willing to grow.

Interpreters of the Christian religion sometimes emphasize the role of either decision or growth to the virtual exclusion of the other. Some focus on a particular time and place when they decided to "turn their lives over to God." They are concerned with the particular moment of conversion or commitment and often dismiss talk about growth or pilgrimage as vague and wishy-washy. But, as we have seen, others are unable to point to such a moment of decision in their experience. If they have grown in their belief in God, it has been by a slow, uneven process that is never quite complete. Such people may regard the idea of a once-and-for-all decision as a distant possibility, or they may reject the notion entirely as being too simplistic to reflect the vagaries and subtleties of experience.

What is often lost in drawing such distinctions is that it poses a false choice. Both decision and growth have a place in relationships, including our relationship with God. This is easy to observe in matters of the heart. There is a place for the slow flowering of a love, but there is also a place for the decision to marry. We may not be able to decide to love someone, but we can decide to commit ourselves to the one we have begun to love. Further, we may find that our commitment to another allows our love for that person to increase as nothing else can. Likewise, in our relationship with God, it is important to recognize that there is a place for the slow growth of belief, but it is equally important for us to grant the place of decision. Here too growth and decision are not unrelated. It can be in living out the implications of our commitment to God that our beliefs can ripen and flourish.

We have already seen that those who seek to overcome their doubts about God cannot do so through a sheer exercise of the will. We cannot decide to believe in God. Rather, belief is given to us. And most often belief is a gift that is given in increments. Belief may grow dramatically at certain times, but more often the growth of belief is gradual, almost imperceptible. But this does not mean that the will plays no role in the development of belief. Indeed, the proper exercise of the will is very important for the person who seeks to believe or believe more fully. We cannot decide to eliminate our doubts, but we can decide to act in spite of them. In the terms used in the last chapter, it is by an act of the will that we can decide to wait actively for belief.

Again, we should remind ourselves of the distinction between belief and faith. If we cannot choose to believe in God, we can still entrust ourselves to God through faith. Our own determined efforts are not enough to decrease the scope and depth of our doubts, but we can put our faith in God, in spite of those doubts. We cannot choose to have the convictions of the confirmed believer, but we can choose to act like those who believe in God. That is, through faith we can commit ourselves to the worship and service of God in the hope that, in time, we will come to believe more fully in the God we have been worshiping and serving.

The Difficulty of Commitment

Nevertheless, even in those times when the necessity for decision is pressed on us, when we are presented with the simple choice of saying yes or no to the Christian God and can no longer defer a commitment by citing our doubts, there are powerful enticements to saying no. Even if we were not considering weighty religious matters, this generalization holds true: It is more difficult to say yes to something than it is to say no. It is more difficult to get up and dance than it is to stay seated and watch. After all, if we affirm something, give a big rousing yes, we will be asked to defend ourselves. But if we say no to something, we are not so vulnerable to criticism.

I learned this lesson rather painfully from my own experience. One year in divinity school, I took a course in dramatic criticism at the Yale School of Drama. It was an upper-level seminar taught by a famous critic. In the class were all the people who were studying for their doctorate in dramatic criticism. Then there was I. Now talk about a rough bunch! We were required to view and critique a play each week. And woe unto the poor plays we would attend. Routinely, we would see a play, tear it to shreds in class, and enjoy the whole process immensely.

One day I wrote an appreciative and positive review of a play that everyone else hated with their usual passion. One member of the class responded, "What? You actually liked that vapid bit of fluff?" Another asked, "How could you listen to that actress caterwauling?" Still another chimed in, "How could you even stay awake? I fell asleep right after the grand-mother said, 'Breakfast is ready!'"—the first line of the play.

I stood my ground, but that day I learned that whenever we say yes to something, even if it is just a play, we had bet-ter be prepared to defend ourselves. Strangely enough, I was never asked to defend my negative reviews. At least 90 per-cent of the reviews shared in that class were negative, unre-lentingly negative. Perhaps that is because we were subjected to a particularly poor theatrical season. Perhaps. But we can also conclude that this almost perfect record of negativity can be attributed to the fact that it is easier to say no. We are less likely to be asked to defend a negative comment. If we avoid the commitment of affirmation, we are not such an easy target for criticism.

Now, if it is difficult to stand up for a play in a criticism class, how much more difficult it is to dance for Jesus in a hos-tile world. To entrust ourselves to God and determine that we will follow Jesus is harder, much harder, for then we are no longer committing ourselves to something meager. Rather, we are committing ourselves to something that reaches into every aspect of our lives and has implications further than the

eye can see. And that is difficult. It takes a measure of courage. After all, at some time or other, those who are committed
to the Christian God will be asked to interpret some nook or
cranny of the Bible. They will be asked to defend those who
attend church and why they seem to be such garden-variety
unrepentant sinners. They will be asked the unanswerable
questions of how they can believe in a loving God when the
world is ravaged by evil and suffering.

How difficult it is to respond to these questions, and many
others, especially when we are so keenly aware that we may
have as many doubts as the person asking them. It is almost
impossible to respond to such questions without becoming
open to some fierce accusations. If, on the one hand, those who
have put their faith in God offer an expression of doubt in the
process of responding to such questions, they will be accused
of being hypocrites. If, on the other hand, they respond by
testifying to their beliefs, they will be accused of being self-
righteous. No wonder we avoid such a commitment, if in the
process we can avoid such questions and accusations. How
much easier it is to remain on the sidelines.

Perhaps we have all heard these criticisms of those who
have given a yes to the Christian faith:

- They are too dogmatic. / They are too wishy-washy.

- They are too timid. / They are too militant.

After recognizing this strange mixture of criticism, G. K. Ches-
terton said with sarcasm, "I could only conclude that if Christianity was wrong, it was very wrong indeed!"

But note: If they are skillful enough, critics of those who
have said yes to the Christian faith may never have to tell others what they are committed to themselves. They will be too
busy saying why they cannot be committed to the Christian
God. They may say, and say again, why they cannot entrust

themselves to the object of another's faith, but they will not be caught making any far-reaching commitments themselves. That is too dangerous. It is too comfortable and safe to remain in their seats.

At some point those who remain uncommitted may have to admit that it is not that they are waiting for the right tune. It is that they do not want to dance! For such fussy dancers there is only self-imposed exile on the edge of the dance floor. They may be safe, but they will never know the joys of dancing. Even those reluctant middle school folk will learn this when they finally venture onto the dance floor: The music always sounds better on the dance floor than it does from the sidelines.

We may wish that the power and allure of the Christian faith were obvious to the observer. But it is not. To grasp the Christian faith, or to be grasped by it, it must be lived, not merely observed. The Christian faith is understood only from the inside. Only by living the Christian faith can we hope to see the truth and attractiveness of it.

We may reach the point where we are willing to give the Christian faith a bit of a try, attend a few worship services, read a book or two, try our folded hands at prayer. That is, we may be willing to try the Christian faith much as we may try out fishing or oil painting for a few weekends to see if it appeals to us. We want to taste it before we decide to make a full meal of it. We want our toe to tell us that the water is fine before we plunge in head first. It is not difficult to understand or appreciate why we prefer caution to headlong commitment. But if we let ourselves become satisfied with only such small and tentative steps, the larger satisfactions of the Christian faith may continue to escape us. The attractiveness of Christianity is seldom revealed in a small sample. Those who hold back from more complete involvement and fuller commitment likely will remain primarily observers and will experience the observer's difficulty in understanding and appreciating the Christian faith.

A woman I know finally agreed to give flying a try. She said on her return: "Well, it was all right, but I never really trusted the thing. I never really let my weight down." This woman's experience may only lead her to conclude that she prevented the aircraft from crashing by keeping her body suspended an inch above the seat cushion. Obviously, with such an attitude she will never discover the trustworthiness of aircraft. In a similar way, we must decide to put our trust in God fully before we can discover that God is fully worthy of our trust. It is only by acting in spite of our tentativeness, by "really letting our weight down," that we can learn for ourselves the truth of what we may have heard about God's faithfulness to those who trust in God.

This is not to deny that our belief in God can increase in small stages. What is more, such incremental growth can take place before any decision to entrust ourselves to God. But those who want to experience the full truth and strength of the Christian faith must eventually decide they will live within it. They cannot merely sample it like a prospective hobby or put a dab on their plate like a morsel from the smorgasbord table. If they aim to grow into a full and mature belief, they must eventually decide to live a life of faith. For those whose hearts are restless, whose belief is enough to tantalize but not enough to satisfy, the moment of decision is extremely important. Still, we would prefer to avoid it. The necessity for decision will almost always be presented to us earlier than we might expect or like. We will likely want to protest that we do not feel ready. Yet for those who are eager to grow in their belief, the time for commitment can be postponed, but it cannot be avoided. Without it, growth in belief can be forever stunted.

To be sure, not everyone is in a position to make such a decision. For some the step of faith is still impossible. In some instances the tentacles of doubt have such a powerful grip that they hold the person back. Yet others may claim that their doubts make commitment impossible when in fact their doubts make commitment necessary, for it is only by boldly stepping out in faith that they can find those doubts diminished.

Choosing the Life of Faith

When, then, can we consider ourselves ready to make such a commitment? How can we know when the time for decision has arrived? It will not be when our belief is firm, when all questions are resolved. It will not be when the decision comes easily, without effort or second thoughts. Rather, it is when we are willing to view our old doubts in a new context, the context of a life of faith instead of a life free from any such commitment. It is when, for reasons that may remain a mystery, we find we are willing to follow our tapping toe onto the dance floor even though other parts of us would prefer to sit resolute and comfortable in a chair the whole evening. It is when we find ourselves willing, for once, to act on the great "perhaps." Camus's comment that there are times when we must make a 100 percent commitment to that about which we are only 51 percent certain is not always helpful in such matters because belief is not always accorded the luxury of even so meager a majority. Sometimes all we can muster is a small fraction of belief, far short of a majority, and yet we can still be willing to act on it. The majority need not rule. Giving our doubts free rein is different from allowing those doubts to reign as king.

Once we have decided to entrust ourselves to God through faith, what then? The implications are far-reaching, but they may not be immediately evident. Doubt will still gnaw and pester. Perhaps doubt and belief still will be found in the very same proportions as they were before any such commitment. We should not expect otherwise. The critical question, however, is not whether we still have doubts but whether we will allow those doubts to keep us from acting in trust. A character in Shakespeare observed, "Our doubts are traitors and make us lose the good we oft might win by fearing to attempt." But we do not have to let our doubts paralyze us, traitors though they be. After all, the great exemplars of faith are not those who were free from doubt but those who acted in spite of their doubts.

We sometimes imagine that it can be otherwise. For instance, we might picture Columbus as confident and certain as he set out on his famous voyage, disdainful of those who warned him that he would sail to the end of the flat earth and simply fall off. Certainly it was not so unambiguous as that. If we fully consider what it meant to attempt such a voyage, we can imagine Columbus on the ship's bridge looking out over the horizon, thinking to himself, "It does look rather flat after all. Uh-oh. Could that be the edge right there?" Of course Columbus had doubts! It would take a fool not to have them. But, again, the critical question is this: Did he turn back? Did his doubts keep him from commitment? Did his doubts paralyze him or did they just add a dimension of adventure to his journey?

Eventually Columbus discovered that his beliefs were well founded but not without some anxious moments along the way. Every new horizon offered new reason for doubt. Rough seas are not the only thing that can turn an explorer green. Nevertheless, even if Columbus could not silence his "traitorous" doubts, he knew that he did not have to give in to them. And those who set out on a voyage of faith will learn with Columbus that they may think they know something about the land they are attempting to reach, only to discover upon their arrival that it is different from anything they have yet experienced, at once more awesome and strange and wondrous than anything they could imagine, indeed a New World. It is only by remaining committed in the presence of loud and persuasive doubt that such important discoveries are made.

Those who seek to discover a fuller belief in God must be willing to risk commitment in the face of uncertainly. The decision to entrust ourselves to God through faith does not eliminate the need for active waiting. Rather, it is after such a commitment that our waiting for belief can begin in earnest. We do not "practice" the Christian faith in the hope that our practice will one day bring us to the point where we can take such a bold step. Rather, we take such a bold step in the hope that we can "practice" the Christian faith in all its dimensions. It is a fearsome prospect. Those who approach such a decision with ease are almost certainly foolhardy or naïve. And those who fall into such a commitment easily likely will fall out of it all too easily as well.

Those who understand the implications of such a decision would avoid it entirely were it not for the presence of something even more unrelenting than their doubts. That is the persistent hope and promise of what lies on the other side of the decision, a living relationship with the living God. Such a decision may never be easy, but those who take such a step can do so with the assurance that Pascal said God offers to each of us: "Console yourself, you would not seek Me if you had not found Me."[1]

Questions for Reflection

♦ Jesus uses dance as an image of commitment. In what ways is it an apt image?

♦ In what ways might your own doubts be self-serving?

♦ What, specifically, would you do first if you wanted "to give the Christian faith a try."

CHAPTER SEVEN

A Word to Church Leaders

THIS CHAPTER IS ADDRESSED especially to clergy and other church leaders who want to consider how best to minister to those who have religious doubts. This is not a call for a specialized ministry with one small sub-group within our congregations. It is not a narrow concern. Much depends on the pastor's ability to minister faithfully and effectively to those who doubt. Doubt is as close to being a universal experience as anything in human life. Wherever we may turn the issue arises again, the old questions challenging us in new forms. And the concern is as deep as it is broad. Those who are permitted entry into the private lives of people cannot help but realize that religious doubt is of intimate and profound concern to individuals. The church, like the world at large, is filled with people who are eager, even aching, to have their religious doubts taken seriously.

Seekers Outside and Inside the Church

A landmark Gallup study of religious attitudes in the United States once revealed that a staggering number of people avoid any association with a church because they are convinced they will not find one in which they can explore their religious doubts freely. Over half of the unchurched said that they could foresee becoming "a fairly active member" of a church in the future. And note this: No fewer than 32 percent of these potential members said that "they would be back in the Christian fellowship if they could find a pastor or church friends with whom they could easily and openly discuss their religious doubts."[1]

We might be tempted to respond to this finding with a measure of cynicism. After all, it is easier to respond to a survey than to climb out of bed and go to worship on a Sunday morning. The finding takes on greater significance, however, when we note that this factor ranks dramatically higher than any other cited by the potential church members among the unchurched. As we might expect, a significant number of those who could foresee becoming an active member of a church said they were looking for a church with good preaching. But more than twice as many indicated that they were looking for a church in which they could "easily and openly discuss their religious doubts." Other considerations were cited almost as frequently as good preaching, such as the desire to find a church that is "seriously concerned to work for a better society" or one that has a good church school and youth program. Nevertheless, those surveyed cited no factor with anything close to the frequency as the desire for a community in which their doubts could be explored.

That Gallup study did not attempt to discern if this same desire is felt by a similar proportion of those who are currently active in a church. One of the striking things about the Gallup survey, however, is that it revealed a remarkable similarity between the beliefs and attitudes of those who are currently members of a church and those who are not. We can safely assume that this similarity exists in the desire to share religious doubts. Of course, we hardly need a poll to point this out to us. We know, at least in some general way, that even active church members have doubts. We know, too, that such doubts are not a matter of slight or passing concern. We can be sure that when the unchurched speak so forcefully of their desire to "find a pastor or church friends with whom they could easily and openly discuss their religious doubts," they are voicing the concerns of their counterparts within the church as well.

And, unfortunately, those who are currently outside the church are largely right in their observation that few churches invite and accept such an open expression of doubt. In other words, it is not that those who have joined a church have been successful in their search for a church in which they can express their doubts. More likely, they too have given up on finding this type of fellowship, the only difference being that they have decided to join a church anyway. Perhaps they are reconciled to the fact that they may never find a community in which their searching religious questions will be heard and their profound doubts accepted. But the longing does not cease. This realization is laced with poignancy. We can imagine an active member of a church attending worship as she does almost every Sunday and yet feeling strangely out of place because she fears that her lingering doubts disqualify her. She attends a Bible study class, but in the course of the discussion she is able only to hint at the serious questions that cloud her thought for fear that any more direct expression might shock the pastor and disturb the other participants, whom she assumes have long since resolved such questions in their own minds. When the pastor pays a call after the death of her husband, she cannot bring herself to look at him directly for fear that her eyes will betray the doubts that she dare not utter. All the while she is waiting for the pastor and people of the church to indicate by some word or gesture that they are open and receptive to her real questions, to the person she really is.

If this picture does not describe everyone within our congregations, surely it reflects the experience of many, more than those of us who are church leaders usually let ourselves recognize. It is not that we are loutishly insensitive to the personal struggles of those who doubt. There are always those who are open with their doubts, and we may respond to them with sensitivity. But the presence of those few who express their doubts openly all too easily can lead us to conclude that if such concerns exist they will find expression, when in fact a far larger number may hold similar doubts without expressing them. In most people the struggle with doubt is silent, even invisible. For the most part, those who fill our churches simply do not look like people who are plagued with doubts. They look comfortable in the pew during worship. They do not fidget or wrinkle their brows. After the benediction they greet us cheerfully. In fact, they may give no audible or visible sign whatsoever of the doubts that churn within.

This disparity between outward appearance and inner reality is not prompted by a desire to deceive. Rather, most of those in our congregations want to grow in their belief and hope that they can do so through participation in a church. But most people simply do not know how to go about expressing their doubts, and most churches lack an inviting environment in which people can do so. If people receive no clue of the doubts held by those they encounter within a church, they may conclude that others are free from doubts, and it then becomes exceedingly difficult for them to voice such doubts themselves. Without any acceptable alternative in sight, many keep their doubts to themselves and merely reflect the outward behavior of others who feel equally unable to express their doubts.

Although this is a tragic circumstance, it has some of the dynamics of a playful trick my friends and I liked to play on unsuspecting adults when I was a boy. It went like this: We would stand on a woodland path and find a particularly unremarkable spot just a few feet away, an area with, say, a dead tree and some mud and dried leaves. When we heard some adults coming we would stare at this area with delight and amazement. Then we would assume our most awestruck voices and say things like, "Can you believe that?" "What do you think it is?" "I'm not sure, but it is undoubtedly the most remarkable specimen I have ever seen!" "I can't wait to tell my parents about it!" By this time the adults were close enough to pick up on our excitement and soon they would be staring over our shoulders, trying to see what all the commotion was about. After a good long while they would usually ask, "What do you see?" Of course, we would never let on that we did not see much of anything ourselves. Instead, we would reply, "Don't you see it? It's right in there!" When the adults still did not confess to seeing anything, we would say with some barely masked impatience, "Well, if you can't even see what we're talking about, what good would it be for us to tell you what it is?" More than once the victims of our prank became so exasperated that they would eventually say, "Oh yes. I do think I see it now," and be on their way. I am persuaded that many within our churches feel like those unfortunate adults. They are surrounded by those who seem to be pointing to the reality of God, and though they themselves do not see it with certainly and may not see it all, they do not want to appear foolish. It is easier to go along and leave doubts unexpressed.

The Church's Receptiveness to Doubters

Throughout this book it has been stressed that for those who want to believe or believe more fully, it is important to act out the Christian faith. Often a person must do what a believer does before he or she can believe what a believer believes. Nevertheless, it is important to stress that this needs to be done within a trusting and accepting environment in which doubts can be freely expressed. On the one hand, if people are only given an opportunity to act out the Christian faith but are unable to share their doubts, they will come to feel isolated among people with whom they do not seem to belong. They may conclude that their continued participation in Christian practice is nothing short of dishonest. On the other hand, those who are given ample opportunity to express their doubts but at the same time are not encouraged to act out the Christian faith can become endlessly adrift in a sea of doubts. Every question leads to another. Their doubts and questions occupy them so completely that they do not live the Christian faith long enough to see the truth in it. Consequently, the two must be done together: People need both to act out the belief they cannot yet claim and to talk out the doubt they cannot yet escape.

If worship is planned and led with care, it can strike both notes and thus set the proper tone for the life of a church that aims to minister to those with doubts. In worship, people are given an opportunity to act out belief. They can practice the Christian faith by praying, singing, confessing, and taking part in other communal expressions and experiences. Further, through the preaching of the church, they can better learn how to integrate Christian practice into other aspects of their lives.

As the central activity of a Christian church, however, worship also plays a critical role in shaping a community in which doubts can be freely expressed. This is not achieved by reducing the historic affirmations of the church to those things that are easily believed. Nor is it done by diluting the gospel until it becomes what C. S. Lewis called "Christianity and water." Rather, it is achieved by giving voice to the full power and scope of the gospel while at the same time finding a variety of ways to recognize the reality of doubt about those very things that are expressed. When people have the question that Karl Barth said everyone brings to worship ("Is it true?"), they need to hear the ringing affirmation that, indeed, the gospel is true. But for many, to entertain the truth of the gospel, they also need to have recognized what they know all too well: It *seems* unbelievable. If we do not freely grant this from the very beginning, our response to the question "Is it true?" may never be heard. If, however, we can begin by affirming together that the gospel does indeed appear unbelievable, we have an opportunity to affirm that it is true in spite of appearances. It is ironic that if the gospel is to be believed, we must first grant that it seems unbelievable. If, with Paul, we are to accept the wisdom of Christ, we must first recognize that it does indeed appear foolish. The perception that the gospel appears foolish needs to be affirmed in order that the truth of the gospel may be received.

William Muehl, former professor of preaching at Yale Divinity School, has given this charge to many seminarians: "Always remember that most of the people you face on a Sunday morning almost decided not to come." We might interpret that statement as a simple reminder that people will be drawn to worship if preachers give lively and engaging sermons, spiced with liberal doses of amusing stories. But Muehl's charge implies much more. The reason that many almost decide not to come to worship is not that they suspect that they will not be sufficiently entertained. Rather, they anticipate that the range of their deepest concerns, including their doubts, will not be addressed. Thus they themselves will not feel addressed. They fear that because their most profound needs, including the need to overcome doubt, will not be recognized, they themselves will not be recognized. There is no better way, possibly no other way, to help people feel as if they belong in worship than to speak to their real concerns and needs. They will join us in worship when we start speaking to them as people we know.

If preaching is to respond to the real concerns and needs of those in the congregation, there are times when the subject of doubt needs to be addressed head-on. In taking on such a subject, preachers must draw on all the skill, sensitivity, and inspiration available to them. Worshipers will listen with unusual care to such a sermon. After all, it is a subject of intense personal interest. They believe but want help with their unbelief. They long to be addressed by someone who demonstrates a depth of understanding about these profound and intimate concerns. This is not achieved by responses to the presence of doubt that are pat and filled with easy reassurances. It is important to tell people that doubt is natural, but that is not sufficient, anymore than it is sufficient to tell those who are suffering from a painful disease that the disease and the pain are natural. At the same time, if pastors are to take seriously the doubts that people bring to worship, they must avoid simple prescriptions. If they merely offer a few suggestions about how to overcome doubt, the homiletic equivalent of "Take two aspirins and you'll feel better in the morning," such glib advice will be dismissed as clearly insufficient to fight off the looming presence of doubt. The person who experiences doubt knows that it is not easy; if it were, doubt would have been banished long ago.

If the preacher's words about doubt are to be helpful, or heard at all, they must demonstrate an intimate understanding of the reality and power of doubt. Such understanding is not achieved by using the pulpit as a confessional where the preacher's own doubts become the subject of concern. If the preacher's own doubts are to be shared in a sermon, it is best that they be shared sparingly and with great care. This is not to say that preachers must present themselves as people without doubts. Rather, such doubts are more appropriately expressed in other settings. All too often expressions of doubt within the sermon—sometimes offered as a prelude to facile testimony about how such challenges have been overcome in the preacher's own life—are nothing more than a gratuitous attempt to show that the preacher is a regular person with the usual human concerns. And, if such expressions of personal experience with doubt are not gratuitous, if they are genuine and impassioned, they can all too easily distract listeners; the preacher's own doubts, rather than the gospel or the concerns of the worshiper, become the focus of interest.

Nevertheless, preachers can demonstrate an intimate understanding of doubt by other means. They can speak from an experience of doubt without speaking directly about that doubt. They can speak of doubt with such a depth of understanding and concern that it is obvious they know very well the ways of doubt. They can speak as people who know the complex and subtle shape of doubt and the various ways in which it can hold a human heart in its grip. They can do this by addressing the subject of doubt with such clarity that among the things that becomes clear is that they too have experienced it. All this can be achieved without speaking of the preachers' own doubts or making them the focus of concern in their preaching.

Obviously, an occasional sermon on the subject of doubt is not a sufficient response to such a profound and pervasive concern. Instead, preachers need to be mindful of the doubts held by those they address no matter what text they use or subject they consider. Some churches have hired a "resident theologian" to live and work with a local congregation and to educate the members in the ways of faith. It strikes me that it might be even more fruitful to hire a "resident skeptic" to work with the preacher in the preparation of sermons. The task of the resident skeptic would be to help the preacher avoid easy assumptions about the beliefs of those he or she addresses. The resident skeptic would stand over the shoulder of the preacher in study and pulpit and whisper in the preacher's ear annoying questions like these: "Is it really that easy?" "Is it as simple as that?" "Yes, you've said that many times, but how do you know it is true?" If preachers would listen to such resident skeptics and respond to the questions they raise, I am convinced the result would be sermons that would have a clarity, power, and effectiveness that is so often lacking. But, of course, it is not necessary to put a resident skeptic on the payroll of the church because there are already skeptics residing in each congregation and indeed each person. All that is required is that preachers sufficiently remember or imagine their concerns and do their best to address them.

People long to be taken seriously, which may mean more than, but can mean nothing less than, that they long to have their doubts taken seriously. If preachers can demonstrate through their preaching that they take seriously the doubts of those they address, the gospel will then have a full and blessed opportunity to do its mysterious, transforming work. When their words reveal that they understand the doubts that can gnaw at the human spirit, an opening is created. It is an opportunity to speak the truth and, for once perhaps, to have it fully heard. Something of enduring power can happen when words of hope and affirmation are expressed without flinching or backing away in the presence of clearly recognized doubt. When expressions of faith are offered in this context, people no longer need to fear that such words of faith will wither and blow away like dead leaves as soon as they are exposed to the strong and random winds of doubt. If worshipers sense that preachers know the strength and scale of their doubts, they may be ready as never before to entertain the affirmations of belief that follow. Once people know that preachers understand their despair, they may be prepared to hear words of hope. If they sense that their most profound needs are understood, they may be in a position to entertain the possibility that the gospel being preached addresses those needs. If they are convinced that pastors recognize their real questions in all of their nagging force, they may be open to the answer offered. It is a precious opportunity, an opportunity to be seized. It is an opportunity that comes when pastors exercise enough care and sensitivity to note the reality of doubt in the lives of those to whom they preach.

Encouraging the Expression of Doubt

Then, too, as has been shown, it is important to give people an opportunity to express their own doubts within an open and trusting environment. Clergy or other church leaders may like to think their churches are replete with such opportunities, but an honest assessment will likely reveal something else. That such opportunities are rare is all too clear when church leaders try to specify just where in the life of their churches no assumptions are made about the beliefs of those who participate and where expressions of doubt are not only expected but invited. Most Bible study groups do not create such an environment. Even many church discussion groups that are considered open and freewheeling include the clear though perhaps unexpressed understanding that some opinions are improper and some doubts too unseemly to be shared openly.

Before people can be helped with their doubts, they must first be helped to express those doubts. Only rarely is such an environment created without the intention and concerted effort to do so. The participants in church study or discussion groups often view their own doubts as rare, if not sordid, and take it for granted that others do not struggle with similar concerns. And those who lead such groups often assume that if doubts are powerful enough they will find some expression when, in reality, those doubts can be so powerful that they cannot be expressed without invitation.

Nevertheless, an open and trusting environment can be created in which doubts can be shared and explored. It might take the form of a small, ongoing study or discussion group to which people are invited if they promise to bring their doubts with them. It is important that receptivity to doubt be stated from the beginning. For some people, it is only when they know that their doubts are invited that they will feel truly invited themselves. Once such a group has gathered, it is necessary to find a variety of ways to indicate again and again that it is not only assumed that the participants brought doubts along but also that it is appropriate to express them. Again, the voicing of doubt needs to be invited, even encouraged. And when doubt finally finds its voice, be it a whisper or shout, tenuous or violent, it is essential that such expressions be affirmed and accepted. Pastors should not be too quick to try to respond. There will be time later for counter-arguments and affirmations of belief but not now.

It can be difficult to let expressions of doubt stand without response, even if it is just temporarily. If pastors accept Jesus' description of himself as "the Truth," they will want to give testimony to this affirmation. But if they do so too quickly, while people are just beginning to give their doubts full and honest expression, they can unwittingly give the impression that, if Jesus is the truth, he is only a half-truth, fearful of investigation, hiding behind a version of the Fifth Amendment, lest he incriminate himself. The willingness to accept the doubts people share without giving an immediate response demonstrates an understanding that the truth of Christ can stand up to thorough examination.

Then too, pastors may respond to every doubt as it is expressed because they can see that people are burdened by their doubts and the pastors want to provide prompt relief. Relief is not achieved by responses that are precipitous. On the contrary, if pastors respond to every doubt as it is expressed, they may discourage the kind of honest sharing that can be most helpful. They may fully understand the questions people have and believe they have answers to offer, but people often need to spend time with their questions before any answer can be heard. Usually people are more impatient with easy answers than they are with leaving their questions open for a time. Pastors need to allow people to speak in their native language first, the language of doubt, before they can expect them to be conversant in the language of belief. That means that, if pastors are to communicate with those who doubt, pastors must speak that language themselves. If they insist on speaking only the language of belief, their words will be as vain as the words of the tourist who does not speak the language of a foreign land but who assumes that if he speaks louder and slower he will be understood. There are many ways in which God's name can be taken in vain, but surely one way is to speak repeatedly of God's power and love before people have had an opportunity to share their doubts about such affirmations. In such instances, God's name indeed can be uttered in vain.

Besides, most people have already heard what pastors will have to say. It is likely, however, that they have never had the experience of having their doubts fully heard and accepted. When they have expressed their doubts and, especially, if they hear that others present share similar concerns, they may be able to hear the pastor's words of promise with new ears. This takes time. Pastors cannot rush people through their doubts. There is no efficient way to firmer belief and diminished doubt.

But if pastors take great care to understand people's doubts and if they can demonstrate that they understand them, affirmations of belief can then be expressed with conviction, and even boldness. The gospel has an unusual opportunity in such circumstances. It may be expressed no differently than it has been on other occasions, but it will be heard differently. Although pastors may respond directly to some of the doubts that are expressed, they need not parry every doubt. Rather, if they have listened to doubts with care, they can simply set the affirmations of faith in the midst of the expressions of doubt. They can let the gospel speak for itself in the hope and expectation that it will be heard anew. They can proclaim the gospel with something like abandon. They can set the gospel loose so that it can work its own miracles by its own gracious and mysterious means.

And, of course, pastors will be surprised by where the gospel will take hold. I learned this one summer while working as a youth minster in a small rural church. One of my responsibilities was to work with the young people while their parents were in worship. The assignment was simple: I was supposed to teach the gospel to the children, age seven to seventeen, and keep them all interested at once. Anxious to please, somewhat embarrassed by the unmistakable wetness behind my ears, I faced twenty expectant, enthusiastic—and screaming—children.

I was armed only with an idea: Each week during that hour the group would act out a different parable, and in this session, our first together, we would act out the parable of the sown seeds. We would plant a bean seed by the side of the road, on rocks, among thorns, and in fertile soil. In the succeeding weeks the children would check the seeds to note their progress. In a few weeks the beans that were planted by the side of the road, on the rocks, and among the thorns would all have died, while the bean that was sown in the good soil would be a plant laden with beans. The meaning of the parable would be clear to all, and the children would skip home to sin no longer. Or so went the plan.

At first everything seemed to be following schedule. The beans were planted as prescribed. We discussed the significance of each location and why we could expect that the seed planted in the good soil would be the only one to survive.

As the weeks passed I noticed with horror, the children with glee, that the bean that had been planted among the thorns was keeping pace with the bean that had been planted in fertile soil. In four weeks only one plant remained—the one among the thorns. In fact, it seemed to be thriving. A few weeks later the plant was doing so well it yielded a handful of beans. The children planted one of the beans in an earthenware pot and gave it to me as a gift. I thanked them cordially, though that bean never sprouted because, for some dark and mysterious reason, I forgot to water it.

That summer I had started out to teach one lesson and ended up learning another lesson entirely. The parable teaches us that some people are more receptive than others to the word of God. But what I noticed, only after attempting to act out the parable, is that Jesus never suggested we should pass up the rocks and thorns of this world to look for more accommodating ground. The reason is this: We never know, cannot know, where the rocks are, where the good soil is. That knowledge is given to God alone.

In Christian ministry this lesson is repeated in countless ways. We pastors simply do not know where the word of God will take hold. If we allow people to express their doubts fully, we may be shocked by the power of what we see. We may despair of the gospel ever taking root in lives so cluttered with doubts. We, who judge by appearances, might even pass up those who are so full of doubt, thinking they are not ready for the word of God, assuming that their doubt will surely choke whatever tender growth in belief that might spring forth. But we are asked to spread the gospel even in those lives that seem least promising. That thorny person, despite all appearances, may be ready for the word of God.

We cannot create listeners. We can only spread the gospel. We cannot determine where a seed will sprout. We can only plant and water the seeds we have been given.

Could I be the only one who feels a certain disappointment in that realization? After all, it means that our role as ministers and preachers may be more limited than we sometimes like to imagine. When described in this way, our role sounds decidedly unprofessional. It seems to put our work in the category of common labor: Can we not, at the very least, think of ourselves as landscape architects? We want to be able to do a little soil analysis and chart crop yields, something more exacting and precise, something that can be done in a technician's white coat, rather in torn and muddy overalls.

There is a certain sadness here as well, for if we pastors are mere planters and waterers, we will never be very good judges of our own success. After all, we are more like itinerant farmhands, sowing and watering where we do not reap. Or perhaps it is as if we plant seeds in the dark, hoping, praying that some growth is taking place, perhaps at times almost hearing something grow, but never seeing the growth in its full shape and color.

There is frustration here as well. If the mystery and majesty of God's love means anything to us, it is something we want to impart to others. Wanting to impart the mystery, we ask how it can best be done; we don the technician's white coat and seek techniques. The frustration comes when we realize that such efforts always seem to fall short. We may enjoy something like success in one instance, but it proves illusory as we find that we are unable to repeat it. Even the most carefully crafted sermon cannot diminish doubt. Even the most skillful planting does not avail with soil that is not ready. Only God can do those things. We cannot impart the mystery any more than we can make a plant grow by giving it encouraging words. In the end, we can only admit that we are not imparters of the mystery, but merely witnesses to it and, occasionally at least, channels for it.

But if there is disappointment, sadness, and frustration in seeing ourselves as such limited partners in God's work, there is also joy in that realization as well. As spreaders and waterers, common laborers, we can enjoy a certain abandon. In our preaching and teaching we can spread the gospel with confidence, even among people who are so filled with doubt that they do not appear ready for the word we share. Of course, we are called to preach and teach with passion, and even something approaching skill, but in so doing we can leave to God the exacting work of shaping a human soul. What a freeing realization that is!

When the good news is spread in this manner, not only will we be surprised by joy, but we will know the joy of surprise as well: We simply never know where the word of God will grow, for it can grow and flourish in the most unlikely places, even in the midst of great doubt. We will know the joy of surprise if we recognize that the gospel has a power beyond anything we can say or do. The gospel has a life of its own, and thank God—for if it were up to us, we would certainly choke it. If people could be freed from doubt by any sure human means, that is, if communicating the gospel were a technique, we would certainly misunderstand the technique or misuse it.

But, sometimes, and we are often the last ones to sense it, something grand speaks through even our most stumbling efforts to communicate the gospel. A sapling grows in the cracks of a sidewalk and our response can only be wonder and delight. Belief springs robust in the midst of doubt, and we understand once again that God is more powerful than doubt. Then we will remember the words, "The light shines in the darkness and the darkness has not overcome it," and we will see that those words are true, after all.

Questions for Reflection

- In your church is there a presumption that the people who gather for worship already have faith?

- Does your church allow, or even encourage, the expression of doubt?

- In your church, how do people respond when someone expresses his or her doubts?

- Can you think of an example of being surprised by where the word of God took hold, either in your life or in the life of another?

Notes

Chapter 1

1. John H. Westerhoff III, *Will Our Children Have Faith?* (Minneapolis: Winston-Seabury Press, 1976), 22.

2. For a discussion of the traditional proofs of the existence of God see Mortimer J. Adler, *How to Think about God* (New York: Macmillan, 1980); John Hick, ed., *The Existence of God* (New York: Macmillan, 1964); Hans Küng, *Does God Exist?* (New York: Doubleday, 1980).

3. Harry Emerson Fosdick, "The Importance of Doubting Our Doubts," a recording of a sermon preached April 12, 1953, in Riverside Church, New York.

4. Baillie as cited in Hick, ed., *The Existence of God,* 15.

5. Westerhoff, *Will Our Children Have Faith?* 126.

6. William James, *The Will to Believe* (New York: Dover Publications, 1956), 5.

7. Lewis Carroll, *The Annotated Alice* (New York: Bramhall House, 1960), 251.

Chapter 2

1. Carroll, *The Annotated Alice,* 251.

2. J. B. Phillips, *Your God Is Too Small* (New York: Macmillan, 1961).

3. Frederick Buechner, *Wishful Thinking* (New York: Harper & Row, 1973), 20.

4. Flannery O'Connor, *The Habit of Being* (New York: Farrar, Straus & Giroux, 1976), 354.

Chapter 3

1. Aiken as cited in Hick, ed., *The Existence of God,* 208.

2. Blaise Pascal, *Pensées* (New York: E. P. Dutton, 1958), 79.

3. Robert Moats Miller, *Harry Emerson Fosdick: Preacher, Pastor, Prophet* (New York: Oxford University Press, 1985), 347.

4. Pascal, *Pensées,* 78–79.

Chapter 4

1. Buechner, *Wishful Thinking,* 51–52.
2. See Carroll, *The Annotated Alice,* 251.

Chapter 5

1. Henri J. . Nouwen, "A Spirituality of Waiting: Being Alive to God's Presence in Our Lives," *Weavings* (January/February 1987): 9.
2. David Everett Roberts, *The Grandeur and Misery of Man* (New York: Oxford University Press, 1955).
3. Rainer Maria Rilke, *Letters to a Young Poet,* trans. M. D. Herter Norton (New York: W. W. Norton, 1962).
4. Mary McDermott Shideler, *In Search of the Spirit* (New York: Ballantine Books, 1985), 86.

Chapter 6

1. Pascal, *Pensées,* 149.

Chapter 7

1. George Gallup, Jr., and David Poling, *The Search for America's Faith* (Nashville: Abingdon Press, 1980), 101. The poll cited here is now over thirty years old. Unfortunately, no subsequent poll asked the same questions, so we cannot know how these attitudes may have changed over the years. We do know, however, that religious doubt is on the rise in America. In a 2012 study the Pew Research Center found that, of respondents under the age of thirty, 31 percent have "doubts about the existence of God." In an earlier Pew study, conducted in 2007, only 17 percent of respondents under thirty reported having "doubts about the existence of God." This seems only to reinforce the case that churches need to find and practice ways to welcome those who entertain religious doubts.